# TRY GIVING YOURSELF AWAY

# TRY GIVING YOURSELF AWAY

*By DAVID DUNN*

SECOND EDITION

---

IN WHICH is set forth that happier way of living which all of us so earnestly seek and so few seem to find ...THIS IS A GREAT PITY since the secret lies within ourselves, and its magic can be enjoyed every day *without price.*

---

Prentice-Hall, Inc.     *Englewood Cliffs, N.J*

LIBRARY OF CONGRESS CATALOG CARD NUMBER 56–9354

Twelfth Printing ...... June, 1967

93243

*TO EVERY MAN AND WOMAN*

*WHO IS SEEKING*

*GREATER HAPPINESS — NOW*

# Table of Chapters

# A book for the times

❧ Several years ago I wrote a brief article entitled *Try Giving Yourself Away*, which appeared anonymously in FORBES MAGAZINE and was reprinted in even more condensed form in THE READER'S DIGEST. With the kind permission of these publishers, and at the request of many persons, I have expanded that short article into the present book, which develops in considerable detail the Art of Giving-Away. In it I have tried to answer many questions that have been put to me by personal friends, and by readers in letters from all over the globe.

These are troubled times. The world is full of strife and heartache. Men and women everywhere seek peace of mind and heart, and wish desperately that they as individuals could do *something* toward lifting the heavy blanket of gloom and fear that oppresses mankind.

Perhaps you and I *can* help. More than anything else, the world needs the healing influence of a great surge of simple *kindheartedness,* to rid humanity of jealousy, selfishness and greed. Such a surge must start with *us,* as individuals; it is beyond the power of the world's rulers or statesmen. In our daily living we average citizens must establish the spirit and set the pattern of a kindlier world.

Could there be a more opportune time for all of us to try giving ourselves away? Could anything else we might do as individuals contribute so much toward the peace of the world, or earn us so much personal happiness? I doubt it.

I invite you to join me in my hobby.

DAVID DUNN

# I make an important discovery

# I make an important discovery

¶ Like most people, I was brought up to look upon life as a process of *getting*. The idea of "giving myself away" came to me by accident. One night, twenty-odd years ago, while lying awake in my berth on the Twentieth Century Limited en route from Chicago to New York, I fell to wondering just where the eastbound and westbound Centuries passed each other in the night.

"That would make an interesting subject for one of the New York Central's advertisements," I said to myself—"Where the Centuries Pass." Whereupon I went to sleep.

Next morning I wrote a letter to the New York Central Lines presenting the idea, "with no strings attached." A few days later I received a courteous letter of acknowledgment and the information that the Centuries were scheduled to pass near the little town of Athol Springs, New York, nine miles west of Buffalo.

Some months later I received a second letter informing me that my "Where the Centuries Pass" idea was to be used as the subject for the New York Central calendar for 1924. You may recall that calendar, a night picture of the oncoming locomotive of one Century and the lighted observation platform of the other, passing on a curve. It was a scene rich in color and railroad romance.

The following summer I traveled extensively. In almost every railroad station and hotel lobby I entered, both at home and in Europe, hung *my* Century calendar. It never failed to give me a glow of pleasure.

It was thus I made the important discovery that anything which makes one glow with pleasure is beyond money calculation, in this humdrum world where there is altogether too much grubbing and too little glowing.

I began to experiment with giving-away, and discovered it to be great fun! My life began to be full of exciting little adventures, and I found myself making many new friends.

I discovered, too, that successful giving-away has to be cultivated. There is a knack to it, just as there is to successful getting. Opportunities for reaping dividends of happiness are fleeting. You have to act quickly or they elude you. But that only adds zest.

One day I woke up to the fact that I was really a collector —a collector of Glows and After Glows. It is a fascinating hobby. Like collecting anything else, you are always looking for new experiences in giving-away to add to your collection. Unlike other forms of collecting, however, you need no safe or cabinet in which to keep your treasures; nor do you have to go out of your way to keep adding to your collection. You have only to look around, wherever you are, to discover some opportunity to give yourself away.

I recommend giving-away as an exciting and thoroughly satisfying hobby. In fact, if you will give it a good try, I'll practically guarantee you a happier life—starting right away!

4

# Chapter 2

# Capsule adventures in giving —and living

¶ Your giving-away will, of course, have to be done in your own individual way, based on the things *you* have to give.

Fortunately each of us has a different assortment of gifts, so there could never be anything standardized about giving-away, even though every one of us were to take up the hobby. Some of us have spare time; others have surplus mental or physical energy; others have a special art, skill or talent; still others have ideas, imagination, the ability to organize, the gift of leadership.

All of us can give appreciation, kindness, interest, loyalty, understanding, encouragement, tolerance — and a score of other little portions of ourselves. Each of us should "major" in the items in which we are "long," and fill in with the others.

Perhaps you will catch the idea faster if I explain how I practice my hobby.

Suppose I am passing a neighborhood store in which I notice a particularly attractive window display. I say to myself, "Someone put real thought into trimming that window, and he or she ought to know that at least one passerby appreciates it."

So I stop in, ask for the manager, and compliment him on the display. I find it always pleases a merchant to know that his windows are noticed, even though I may not buy a penny's worth of the merchandise displayed in them. In one instance the clerk who trimmed the windows received a raise in pay as a result of my compliment.

◆ ◆ ◆

If I particularly enjoy a book, a magazine article, or a play, I write a note to the author, telling him or her of my enjoyment. Sometimes I receive an appreciative acknowledgment; more often I do not. It doesn't matter in the least; I am not collecting autographs; I am just keeping my giving-away machinery in good working order.

◆ ◆ ◆

One Saturday afternoon while working in my garden I thought of an idea which I believed a certain New York department store might find useful. That evening I wrote a letter to the store outlining the idea and presenting it, as is my custom, "with no strings attached." It was adopted with appreciation — and I had acquired a big department store as a friend.

◆ ◆ ◆

If an idea comes to me that I think could be used by a local priest, minister, doctor, lawyer or merchant, I write him a note telling him about it, though he may be a stranger to me.

If in my reading I run across an article, a picture, a cartoon, a poem that I think would interest some friend, or even a casual acquaintance, I clip it out and send it to the person. Sometimes I send clippings to total strangers.

✑    ✑    ✑

One spring evening I stopped at a popcorn wagon in Battle Creek, Michigan. A couple of urchins watched hungrily as the melted butter was being poured on the freshly popped corn. Without seeming to notice the youngsters, I ordered two more bags, paid for them, handed each of the boys his bag, and strode away. This little adventure-in-giving made the world more exciting for four people that evening—for the popcorn vendor, too, enjoyed the episode.

✑    ✑    ✑

The text of an advertisement in a trade magazine appealed to me as being a wonderfully fine piece of writing. I wrote a note to the company saying that, while I was not in the market for their service, I did want to compliment them on their advertisement. Some days later I received a letter from Philadelphia from the man who had written the advertisement. He said my note had encouraged him no end and given him fresh inspiration. I had acquired a new friend in Philadelphia. I have since had many fine letters from him.

✑    ✑    ✑

One evening I was dining alone in a Boston hotel. The selections the orchestra was playing exactly suited my mood. On the way out, impulse prompted me to cross the dining-room to the dais where the musicians were resting between numbers.

7

"Gentlemen," I said, "I have thoroughly enjoyed your program. Several of your numbers were particular favorites of mine. And you put so much spirit into your playing. I want to thank you."

Their faces broke into smiles, and I left them beaming over their instruments. The rest of my own evening was happier.

¶    ¶    ¶

One Sunday afternoon I fell to thinking of an elderly gentleman in failing health whom I had not seen for a long time.

"Why not surprise him by calling him up?" I asked myself.

"I was thinking of you and I wanted to have a little chat," I explained when he came to the phone. We had an enjoyable five-minute visit.

His wife told me, a few days later, that my call had done more for him than a whole bottle of his tonic. "You know," she explained, "the telephone almost never rings for him any more."

¶    ¶    ¶

Tiny episodes, all of these; but they are collectors' items in my hobby of giving myself away.

You may do such things yourself, quite naturally, without stopping to think of them as "gifts." If so, you are to be congratulated. But, judging from my own experience, I'll wager that you could do more of them, if you would make a real hobby of self-giving. And I'll promise that you'll be happier—in proportion as you give.

Only once in recent years have I violated my giving-away philosophy. In suggesting an idea to a shoe manufacturer I hinted that I would not be averse to receiving a pair of shoes in payment. He liked my idea and sent me a certificate good for any pair of shoes of his manufacture. I selected a smart pair of an expensive last and wore them proudly home.

But I lived to regret my avarice! That particular last was not suited to my foot, and it took my feet months to recover from the damage those shoes did. So now when I give away an idea there isn't even a shoestring attached!

# Chapter 3

# "A portion of thyself"

¶ Ralph Waldo Emerson, that lofty idealist who neverthe-less had a penetratingly practical knowledge of human nature, wrote, "Rings and jewels are not gifts, but apologies for gifts. The only gift is a portion of thyself."

Almost anything in the world can be bought for money—except the warm impulses of the human heart. They have to be *given*. And they are priceless in their power to purchase happiness for two people, the recipient and the giver.

Many letters have come to me from people who want to try giving themselves away, but are timid. They are afraid that their simple gifts-of-the-heart would be laughed at. As one correspondent expressed it, "I have nothing of any im-portance to give to anyone."

This is not true. While you may not think of what you have to offer as being of any particular value, it may fill a need in someone's life. And if it does that, even for a fraction of a minute, it will add that much to the world's happiness. And happiness is one of the greatest gifts within the power of any of us to bestow, particularly in these troubled days when the world is full of fear and suspicion, and men's minds and hearts are anxious.

There are a hundred ways to give a portion of yourself. But they all start from the same spot — *your heart.* The French have a proverb, "He gives nothing who does not give himself."

"A portion of thyself," will, therefore, be your stock in trade if you want to add to the happiness of those around you, and to lead a happier and more exciting life yourself. It is the *spirit,* not the *substance,* which carries warmth.

You need not worry for a second because you lack money or material things. You can give yourself extravagantly if you choose, and reap great happiness from your giving, without reaching for your pocketbook. As Longfellow phrased it, "Give what you have. To someone, it may be better than you dare to think."

❧   ❧   ❧

Indeed, of all the things a person may give, money is probably the least permanent in the pleasure it produces, and the most likely to backfire on the giver. Too often it results in disillusionment, sometimes even in wrecked friendship. If you must give money, bear in mind the wise saying of Miguel de Unamuno: "It is not the shilling I give you that counts, but the warmth that it carries with it from my hand."

A New England man states: "It takes courage to give a small portion of yourself in lieu of some obviously valuable article. But a lively imagination made it possible for me to perceive a great many ways in which I might 'spend myself,' instead of the cash I lacked."

I like the conception of "spending one's self," though I believe over the years one's *spending* turns out to be *investing.*

11

Some time ago I received a letter from a woman berating me bitterly for my article on giving-away. She said her husband was a "giver," that he had given away their money, their food, the children's clothes, and even household articles, until they were living almost in poverty.

I have no patience with such giving. When it comes to money and material things, I believe the needs of one's family should always come first. A person has no right to give away things which belong to others, even in the name of generosity. This book is about giving *yourself*.

You are trying to give pleasure to someone, and you know from experience what trifling things give you pleasure. Such simple gifts as a compliment on your home or your children or your new hat, a note, a telephone call, or a simple act that reflects thoughtfulness or friendly interest, will set you up for an hour, perhaps for a whole day. They are the truest form of giving, because they come from the heart—they are literally a portion of the giver.

Happiness must be sipped, not drained from life in great gulps. Nor does it flow in a steady stream like water from a faucet.

"A portion of thyself" is a sip of happiness, as satisfying as it is costless.

# Chapter 4

# Obey your warm-hearted impulses

❢ The secret of successfully giving yourself away is not so much in calculated actions as in cultivating friendly, warm-hearted impulses. You have to train yourself to obey giving impulses on the instant—before they get a chance to cool. When you give impulsively, something happens inside of you that makes you glow, sometimes for hours.

Frequently impulse-giving results in a new friendship, or leads to an interesting adventure. One afternoon during the wartime gas shortage I was driving up a steep hill on my way home. On the sidewalk was a woman carrying two large bags of groceries. My impulse was to stop and ask if she would like a ride. But it meant stopping on the hillside.

"She probably lives on one of the side streets a block or so up the hill," I told myself. But my giving-self squelched that argument and I pulled over to the curb.

"Can I give you a lift?" I asked.

The woman got in gratefully. She had been obliged to walk two miles to the village for her groceries, since the merchants delivered only twice a week, and company had descended on her unexpectedly. She was just starting the long trek home with her bundles.

13

It turned out that she lived just around the corner from my own home, having moved there very recently. Thus, by obeying an impulse, I made the acquaintance of a delightful new neighbor.

❧   ❧   ❧

Recently I was having dinner on a train. The soup was especially good. On impulse I said to the waiter, "Please tell the chef this mushroom soup is delicious."

The waiter looked surprised, then pleased. So, apparently, was the chef, for when the vanilla ice cream I ordered for dessert was served, it was smothered with crushed strawberries, though they were not on the menu. The chef had obeyed an impulse, too—and surprised me!

You just never can tell *what* will happen when you act on a giving impulse!

❧   ❧   ❧

I am sometimes asked, "When you obey your impulses, aren't you likely to be *too* impetuous and get yourself into embarrassing situations?"

Yes; every so often. But what of it? We are supposed to be getting fun out of life. We lose so much by *not* obeying our impulses that I figure we can afford to take a few risks for the sake of adventure.

❧   ❧   ❧

There is a serious aspect to impulse-giving, too. We never know when some impulse action of ours may mean much in the life of a friend or neighbor.

A young dentist of my acquaintance was struggling along in Boston, trying to build a practice. He had come to the end of his money. One bleak Monday morning in February he decided that he would have to give up his dreams of a professional career in Boston and return to his home town.

That morning one of his friends was passing the brownstone building in which his office was located. At church the previous Sunday he had noticed that the dentist looked depressed. Purely on impulse, he decided to stop in to see him. As he mounted the stairs he met the dentist descending.

"Well, where are you going at this time of the morning?" he demanded cheerily.

The dentist confessed that he was going out to make arrangements to have his equipment shipped to his home town. "I just can't make a go of it here in Boston," he admitted sorrowfully.

Taking the young man by the shoulders, the caller turned him around and marched him upstairs.

"Unlock that door," he commanded. "Turn on the lights —all of them—make this place bright and cheerful. You are not going to give up *now*, after all the months you have invested in this place. Goodbye." And, with a friendly slap on the back, he departed.

That afternoon a woman came in who had been recommended to the dentist by a friend. Over a period of weeks this woman's dental work amounted to $300, and her enthusiastic recommendation brought other patients. The tide had turned. In time the man who was saved from quitting by the impulsive act of a friend on a gloomy morning became one of Back Bay's leading dentists.

One day I received this brief note on feminine notepaper from England:

Today I was in the blues. Domestic affairs were a bit worrying. I sat down at my desk to do accounts, but before beginning picked up *The Reader's Digest* and read your article. "Isn't that nice" was my inward exclamation when I had finished. The blues had vanished and I felt quite cheered. You say "one must act fast, while the impulse is fresh." So I am writing at once to send my appreciation.

This woman could not know that her impulsive note from across the Atlantic would arrive at a time when I was going through a period of discouragement, and that it would cheer me as much as my article had cheered her.

Following is another letter which was inspired by that same article:

My first thought, which from long habit I instantly put out of my mind, was to drop you a note telling you how much I enjoyed your article. Then it occurred to me that I was not obeying that natural impulse that made your article so interesting. It also made me realize something that I hadn't really brought to the front of my mind before. I had always thought of certain friends as being generous, but, after thinking it over, I believe they are really successful people at "giving-away."

The writer of this letter has hit on the truth; giving-away is not a matter of generosity — it is the basis of really successful *living*.

❧    ❧    ❧

George Matthew Adams, in one of his syndicated newspaper articles, suggested that everyone set aside one day a week as Surprise Day, and do surprising little things for his friends.

Why not *every day*? There are plenty of opportunities for surprise-giving if you look for them.

The great virtue of surprise is that, whereas things people expect have already lost much of their power to give pleasure, the tiniest surprise adds fresh zest to living.

This is what makes impulse-giving so exciting, for both the surpriser and the surprisee.

# Chapter 5

# A businessman with a hobby

❡ Some people may give themselves as an expression of un-selfishness. To others it may be a matter of conscience. Still others may cultivate giving-away as a Christian duty—and surely giving yourself is the heart of the gospel of Christ, who gave himself wholly.

I respect all of these motives. But I took up giving-away as a hobby because I found that it made my life more exciting, and broadened my circle of friends. I became a happier person. While it pleases me that other people are made happier, I do not look upon anything I do for them as being my conscientious or Christian duty, or as being unselfish. Unselfishness for its own sake does not particularly interest me. It is rather a goody-goody idea, and smacks of self-righteousness.

But when we take a good look at its opposite—*selfishness*—then unselfishness begins to take on an entirely different aspect. For nobody ever found real and lasting happiness in being completely selfish—not in the whole long history of the world. It seems to be a law of life that we enrich ourselves most when we *give* ourselves most fully and freely.

Selfishness, on the other hand, is a sort of slow poison. One dose leads to another, until the system becomes so saturated with it that one's whole life becomes bitter and disappointing. Larger doses are tried in desperation, but they fail to produce the desired results. The end is disappointment.

Giving-away rids the system of the poison of selfishness, and produces a healthy glow that warms the spirit.

So I refuse to be considered "unselfish" or "generous" or "self-sacrificing." I am just a businessman with a hobby.

❧   ❧   ❧

If you are not already an enthusiastic giver-away, perhaps this hobby is just what you need to fill your life with interest and adventure.

If you do take it up in a serious way, let me give you two good starting rules:

First: Never forget that the *little* giving-impulses are as important as the *big* ones—more important in a way, for they help you to form the *habit* of giving yourself away. And until this becomes second nature, your hobby will not pay its fullest dividends.

Second: Start your giving-away as early in the morning as possible. Days are short and the earlier you warm up your spirit and get it "turning over," the more people you will have made happy by the time you tumble into bed at night—and the more exciting your day will have been.

# Chapter 6

# Bread upon the waters

❡ It did not take me long, after I took up giving-away as a hobby, to discover that it is virtually impossible to give yourself away without getting back more than you give—*provided you give away with no thought of reward*. As Seneca, the Roman philosopher wrote, "There is no grace in a benefit that sticks to the fingers."

Usually the return comes in some wholly unexpected form, perhaps long after you have forgotten the giving-away episode.

For example, one Sunday morning an important special delivery letter was delivered to my home, though it was addressed to me at my office and the post office would have discharged its obligation by attempting to deliver it there. I wrote the postmaster a note of appreciation.

More than a year later I was in pressing need of a post office box for a new enterprise I was starting. The clerk at the window told me there were no boxes available, that my name would have to go on a long waiting list.

I appealed to the assistant postmaster, who told me the same thing. As I started to leave, keenly disappointed, the postmaster appeared in the doorway of his adjoining office.

He had overheard the conversation and my name had caught his ear.

"Are you the David Dunn who wrote us that nice letter a year or so ago about our delivering a special delivery to your home one Sunday morning?" I said I was.

"Well, you don't know what a letter like that means to us. We usually get nothing but kicks. You are certainly going to have a box in this post office if we have to *make* one for you."

A few days later I had a box. Bread upon the waters!

❧ ❧ ❧

Without thought of reward, a woman in Alexandria, Virginia, acted on a giving-impulse when a young friend had measles. Realizing that the little girl would be cooped up for some days, she wrote her a series of whimsical letters which she illustrated with clever drawings. Instead of using her own name, she signed the letters "Susie Cucumber," the name of a little fox terrier loved by the neighborhood children.

When she recovered from the measles, the little girl told her friends about the Susie Cucumber letters. Immediately they all wished "Susie" would write to them. Parents, grandparents, uncles and aunts gladly paid for a series of letters. Today this woman does a profitable business on a subscription basis, sending out as many as 100,000 letters a year to children all over the world. A wholly unexpected return on an investment in giving-away.

❧ ❧ ❧

In a letter published in *The Reader's Digest*, R. Webber, Jr., tells of being so impressed with the courtesy of a conductor toward the passengers on a Chicago streetcar that he spoke to him about it when the crowd had thinned out.

"Well," explained the conductor, "about five years ago I read in the paper about a man who was included in a will just because he was polite. 'What the heck,' I thought, 'it might happen to me.' So I started treating passengers like people. And it makes me feel so good that now I don't care if I never get a million dollars!"

That is exactly what I have discovered! Doing what you can to make life more livable for other people makes your own life fuller. Friends multiply and good things come to you from every direction. The world has a way of balancing accounts with givers-away—provided their hands aren't outstretched for return favors.

❧　❧　❧

Thomas Dreier tells the story of a man over eighty who was observed by a neighbor planting a small peach tree.

"Do you expect to eat peaches from that tree?" the neighbor asked.

The old gentleman rested on his spade. "No," he said. "At my age I know I won't. But all my life I've enjoyed peaches— never from a tree I had planted myself. I wouldn't have had peaches if other men hadn't done what I'm doing now. I'm just trying to pay the other fellows who planted peach trees for me."

In practicing giving-away we both plant peach trees and eat peaches, often unconscious of the fruits of our own little thoughtfulnesses, and equally of the thoughtfulnesses others have invested for our benefit, perhaps many years ago.

Today's giving-away is a blind investment in future happiness, though we can never tell when, where or in what form this happiness will come.

Which is part of the fun!

# Chapter 7

# Giving yourself "in kind"

❡ There is a trade term—"in kind"—which applies in a special sense to giving-away. In the old days a farmer might pay his bill at the general store "in kind," that is, in some sort of produce he had raised. Or he might pay his taxes, not in cash, but in hours of labor, working on the township roads.

A gift of ourselves "in kind"—something we can make or do—is often more acceptable to people than anything we might buy for them. We are inclined to value too lightly the gifts "in kind" which we have to offer our friends, neighbors and fellow workers. We take our talents too much for granted.

Within each of us is a great store of giveable riches. It may be in the form of skill of hand, or of some special proficiency or training. It may be the ability to entertain, to organize, to teach. It may be a talent that we have never taken seriously, but which might be cultivated for the pleasure of others. Or it may be a surplus of time.

Failing any of these, what we have to give may be just warmth of heart—and if we think of our hearts rather than our purses as the reservoirs of our giving, we shall find them full all the time!

A gift "in kind" is truly a gift of a portion of oneself.

One Christmas there arrived at our home a box from a farm family. We knew this family lived near no city where they could shop for Christmas gifts. What had they sent us?

Upon opening the box on Christmas morning we found twelve pint jars of home-canned farm products—kernel corn, wax beans, tender little beets, squash, lamb stew, mince meat. No present we received that Christmas was as much appreciated as those twelve pint jars, all neatly labeled in the handwriting of the farmer's wife. They were a gift of herself and her hard-working husband.

⚐   ⚐   ⚐

A fine example of giving one's craftsmanship is the story of A. E. Shaw, a manufacturer of gavels, of Rocky River, Ohio, as told in a copyrighted Associated Press dispatch following the San Francisco meeting of the United Nations.

"I was listening on the radio to the closing session of the United Nations Conference when Stettinius wound it up," Mr. Shaw related. "He pounded the gavel one—two—three times. The first time it sounded all right, but the third time I said to myself: 'That gavel's done for.'"

On a giving-impulse, Shaw wrote Stettinius offering to make him a new gavel. The offer was accepted. The maker of gavels then put his art and his heart into the fashioning of a very fine gavel. He literally gave himself "in kind" to the United Nations.

⚐   ⚐   ⚐

Most physicians, even the famous specialists who command high fees, give their services to deserving people who are unable to pay for medical or surgical care. From others who are well able to pay, they exact substantial fees. In this way they balance their "in kind" giving with their professional getting.

It has always seemed to me that this balancing idea is both wise and fair. I have no patience with so-called generous people who give their time and talents so prodigally that they are a worry to their relatives and friends because they do not earn enough to support themselves and their families. That is unsound "in kind" giving.

We are not all physicians, but many of us earn our living with some talent, skill or craft which we can share on a balanced getting-and-giving basis, charging the world a self-respecting price for our services, but giving ourselves freely "in kind" to worthy causes and deserving individuals who need our help.

Emerson was referring to gifts "in kind" when he wrote: ". . . Therefore the poet brings his poem; the shepherd, his lamb; the farmer, corn; the miner, a gem; the sailor, coral and shells; the painter, his picture; the girl, a handkerchief of her own sewing."

After all, what gift could be so appropriate as a bit of one's own skill of hand or mind?

"You do not have to be rich to be generous," writes Corinne U. Wells. "If he has the spirit of true generosity, a pauper can give like a prince."

Each of us withholds every day a score of little gifts "in kind" that could make our small world, and by multiplication the whole big world, a happier place.

# Chapter 8

# Minutes make fine gifts

❡ Each of us receives an equal allotment of time—twenty-four hours every day of the year. Even the busiest among us has from a few minutes to an hour or more a day which he could give to others in the form of some useful service. Opportunities for time-giving are to be found all around us.

Many of us have a "knack" at something. If we were to use it in our spare time to do things for other people, we would be giving something that perhaps no one else in the world could give quite so acceptably.

A Boston businessman, who was very fond of children but had none of his own, used to stop in at a small home for orphans every Wednesday afternoon between five and six o'clock and entertain the youngsters, giving the matron and her helpers an hour of complete freedom.

He was a big, solemn-faced man, but the children saw right through his dignity. The instant he arrived in the playroom they gathered around him with shouts of joy. In his pocket he would have a bag of hard candy, a packet of picture cards, or some penny trinkets—always just one for each child, which made it all the more precious. Squatting on the floor, he would distribute his treasures, then launch into a story.

27

He was known to the youngsters as The Big Man, for he had stipulated to the matron that his name should be withheld. He wanted none of his business associates to know of his hour with the orphans. "They would think me a sentimental old fool," he explained.

In that hour each week he gave great happiness to a group of fatherless and motherless youngsters, and welcome relief to three overburdened women. "But nobody gets the fun out of it that I do," he always insisted.

He is now dead, but the many boys and girls whose lives he brightened over the years will never lose the memory of The Big Man who gave them an hour of himself every Wednesday, and along with that hour some of his fine character.

Yet many of us would ask, "What really worth-while giving of myself could I do in one hour a week?"

❧   ❧   ❧

A retired railroad engineer, with time on his hands, tends store every day from twelve to one o'clock in a small neighborhood grocery run by a widow who has two small children. While she prepares lunch for her children, he indulges a lifelong ambition to run a grocery store.

"It's the most fun of any hour of the day," he declares. "And handling food for an hour makes me so ravenous that I enjoy my own lunch just about twice as much!"

The truth is, his lunch is seasoned with the spice of giving!

❧   ❧   ❧

An elderly woman of my acquaintance, herself a grandmother, goes every pleasant morning to a certain bench in a city park and watches over from three to half a dozen baby carriages, while the babies' grateful mothers shop or get a hair-do.

❧ ❧ ❧

Another woman in my neighborhood has "adopted" an old lady in a nearby home for the aged. She calls on her once a week, writes her notes between visits, remembers her birthday, takes her and some of her cronies for occasional automobile rides, and loans her books. All in two or three hours a week.

There are many old people, invalids and children in institutions whose lives would be brightened immeasurably if someone would "adopt" them.

❧ ❧ ❧

Hazel I. Dannecker told this story of time-giving in *The Reader's Digest:*

During a long wait in Cincinnati's Union Station, I saw an attractive girl barely in her teens approach a tired young mother with two fretful babies and ask with a friendly smile, "May I look after your children while you rest for a while?"

For nearly an hour the girl entertained the children, then helped the mother to her train. I watched her assist three other harassed mothers, efficiently and tenderly. Finally, during an idle interval, I inquired if she were waiting for a train.

"No," she said. "I live nearby with my aunt and haven't anything to do after school. You see"—and her voice broke —"there were five of us, and when we traveled Mother got so tired. . . . Daddy was in the war. Mother died a few weeks ago.

... She always said I had a way with children. So I come over here and help tired mothers."

↝   ↝   ↝

We are prone to think we have no time to give away because we cannot bank on having spare hours. No matter; minutes, usefully invested, are precious gifts.

During World War II one of the busiest women of my acquaintance kept a steady stream of letters flowing to many service men from her suburban community, whether she knew them well or not. She wrote them the news of their home town, and told them of the doings of the younger set, which she picked up from her own children at mealtime.

Knowing of her strenuous program of war activities, which involved almost daily trips to the city, I marveled at the volume of her G. I. correspondence. One morning I happened to ride to the city with her and she showed me her secret.

Opening her handbag, she exhibited a packet of note sheets and stamped envelopes, a fountain pen, and a list of G. I.'s names and service addresses.

"Whenever I have to wait, even four or five minutes, for a train or an appointment, I address an envelope and start a note," she explained. "Once started, it is easy to add another paragraph the next time I have a few minutes. I average half a dozen letters a day, with seldom as many as ten uninterrupted minutes. And you should see the letters that come back!

"I hesitated to start writing to the boys," she went on to explain, "for fear the things I wrote about would not interest them. But they gave me plenty to write about!"

This last statement has great significance to the would-be giver who lacks imagination as to what he or she may have to give to others. If you *start* to give yourself, be it in ever so simple a fashion, the world will observe your spirit and show you some need that you can supply.

There are a hundred ways of giving away little margins of time you never will miss, which would be riches to someone.

❦   ❦   ❦

I know a busy executive who dictates many letters. Each morning he formulates a short paragraph of personal news or comment outside the realm of business which he has his secretary add, with appropriate variations, to nearly all his letters for the day. As a result, his correspondence has a warmth and friendliness rare in the business world. Yet not a minute of his busy office day does this take, for he formulates the daily paragraph—a bit of himself—on the way to the city on his suburban train.

❦   ❦   ❦

Oddly enough—or perhaps naturally—the busiest people are apt to do the best job of giving-away. They are so busy that they have to obey their giving-impulses *promptly*, and get on with their affairs. Whereas people with plenty of time are likely to debate within themselves: "Shall I, or shan't I?" By the time the debate is over, the opportunity has passed.

❦   ❦   ❦

It is so easy to confuse our daily busyness with our daily business. Many of us earn our living in business, but waste much of the rest of our time on busyness that profits us little.

Time was not created merely to be consumed in working and worrying, rushing for trains, and dashing to appointments. It was intended to be used in "the pursuit of happiness," as our discerning forefathers phrased it in the Declaration of Independence. True, we would find it hard to be happy if we did not work, and earn enough to provide for our families. But beyond that, the aim of all of us should be to *give* and to *get* the greatest possible enjoyment from every sixty seconds of our lives.

In terms of downright happiness, it is my experience that the returns-per-minute from *giving* are far greater than the returns from *getting*.

# Chapter 9

# Multiply your giving by three

❡ You can, if you will, multiply the acceptability of your giving-away by three.

The first multiplier is the *friendly spirit* of your giving. Nearly always the spirit is more important than the gift itself. If it comes from your heart, whether it be a simple "thank you," an enthusiastic note of congratulation, or a tumbler of homemade jelly, it is more acceptable than a costly present given grudgingly or from a sense of duty—which nearly always can be felt by the recipient. The spirit is *you*—"a portion of thyself," as Emerson expressed it.

The second multiplier is the *timeliness* of the gift. Too often we let the moment pass when it is within our power to give some person happiness. A day, an hour, even a few minutes later, the same action will have lost its keen edge of pleasure. That is why impulse-giving has so much to commend it. Your mind and heart take in the situation as it exists at a particular moment in the lives of the people concerned. Your action is tailored to the situation, making it not only well timed but appropriate.

The third—and most potent—multiplier is *enthusiasm*. One reason we get so little excitement out of our daily lives is because we put so little enthusiasm into our hourly living. Whenever we meet a person who is genuinely enthusiastic, it gives us a lift. Such people are givers-of-themselves and are welcome wherever they go, because they make life more interesting. Each of us can do the same for other people.

It takes no great effort, but merely thoughtfulness, to put enthusiasm into your voice in giving-away. When you add enthusiasm, you give people double pleasure, for so few of us put our hearts and eyes and voices into our dealings with those around us. We seem to take it for granted that words are all that are necessary; but words carry only a small part of what we say. The tone in which we say them, if it conveys the warmth of our personality, is much more important than our words.

❧    ❧    ❧

Some of us are undemonstrative because we don't want to be thought "gushers." But it is not necessary to be a "gusher" to be enthusiastic. People who pride themselves on taking everything and everybody matter-of-factly, assuming that other people understand how they feel, would be surprised to find how cold and unappreciative they are thought to be by all but their closest friends.

One man of my acquaintance, who took great satisfaction in never "gushing," told me that at forty-five he was shocked to find that his philosophy of appreciation had been wrong.

"I felt so deeply appreciative for the things people did for me that I was sure they must feel my appreciation," he explained. "But one day I did not get a promotion I had supposed was coming to me. I asked why another man had been chosen for the higher job and was told it was because my superiors thought I silently disapproved of everything and everybody, and with such an attitude I could not be a leader. I investigated further and found that all but my closest friends thought of me as a wet blanket because I never *enthused* over anything."

This man was an absorber of appreciation, but gave none in return, because of a misguided sense of reserve.

◄    ◄    ◄

Here is good news for those to whom enthusiasm does not come naturally: *It can be cultivated.*

At first you must consciously put your eyes, your voice, your spirit—in a word, *yourself*—into your appreciation of people and events and things. Do this around your home, at your work, and in your social contacts, and you will be surprised how quickly it will become second nature. You will find yourself living in a more gracious and enthusiastic world, for your enthusiasm will be reflected back to you from the people to whom you give it.

Spirit—Timeliness—Enthusiasm. These are the three Great Multipliers. They form an important part of the art of giving-away.

# Chapter 10

# The unbuyable gifts

℆ Consider the gifts that money cannot buy, such as kindness, thoughtfulness, courtesy, consideration, and good nature.

Do not misunderstand me: I do not advocate developing a Pollyanna personality. It is just good manners, good morals and good sense to be courteous, thoughtful, kindly, considerate and good-natured. Take kindness, for example.

One night a good many years ago as a Lackawanna ferry nosed into its slip at Hoboken, the passengers in the cabin crowded toward the door—all but one man who was slouched in a drunken sleep.

Perhaps twenty people glanced at the drunkard as they passed. Then one old gentleman went out of his way to step over and shake the sleeper. "Hoboken," he shouted in the man's ear in a kindly tone.

A dozen people turned at the sound of the voice. A look of shame crept into their faces as the whispered word went around that the man who had thought to do what any one of them might have done was Thomas Edison.

"It never occurred to me until I read *Try Giving Yourself Away* that one could adopt simple *kindliness* as a giving-away hobby," wrote a friend.

Why not? Not only is it a fine hobby, but it is a wonderful way to collect friends. It springs *from* the heart and speaks *to* the heart.

❡   ❡   ❡

So, also, does *considerateness*.

Doubtless you are a normally considerate person. I had thought of myself as such. But I was surprised to discover how much *more* considerate I could be by cultivating the habit of projecting my mind, for a tiny fraction of a second, into the mind and heart of every person I encountered. This technique revealed an astonishing number of opportunities to say something or do something that would make some person warmly appreciative.

You can even be considerate silently. A train starts to fill up. Instead of spreading out over the seat to try to keep it to yourself, you can make the vacant space beside you look actually inviting. You will find yourself enjoying your spirit-of-sharing as much as it is appreciated by the fellow passenger who settles beside you in response to your silent hospitality.

❡   ❡   ❡

*Thoughtfulness* is a twin of considerateness.

One of the busiest and most successful professional men in America is the most thoughtful person I have ever known. Just to come into his presence is to experience a sense of being looked after, so many are the little things he does and says that make you feel comfortable, in mind and body. I verily believe, that from the time this man gets up in the morning until he goes to bed at night, he never neglects an opportunity to exercise thoughtfulness, with his family, his patients, his professional associates, his friends, and the strangers he encounters. Yet no one would think of accusing this man of being saccharine. He is not the gushy type; in fact his personality is a bit on the austere side. But he is loved and respected by all who come in contact with him.

❧ ❧ ❧

*Courage* is one of the really rare gifts.

How often, in a group or a meeting, do we see some man or woman take a courageous stand in a situation where a hard decision is required, with the result that the whole group decides aright.

Recently there passed away a member of a board of directors on which I serve. The president of the board paid him this fine tribute: "In all the years Walter served on this board, whenever there was a decision to be made which took courage, he always faced the issue and insisted that we make the *right* decision. He literally gave courage to all of us."

The person who gives his courage indeed gives a worthy gift to his fellow men, and to the world at large.

❧ ❧ ❧

*Good nature* is a gift which brightens the world and reflects back on the giver.

Several years ago a very wealthy man declared that he would give a million dollars for Charles Schwab's quick, good-natured smile. Yet he might have had it for nothing had he but schooled himself to smile in every trying situation—and charge it up to good nature.

A warm, friendly smile is appropriate to any situation. It is a sample of what you are in your heart, so you are literally giving a bit of *yourself.*

A friend who journeyed around the world before the days of world cruises, when native peoples were not used to tourists, told me, "A smile was the one thing the people of every country understood. So I smiled myself around the globe, and made friends in every country—without the services of an interpreter!"

In my own more limited travels abroad I found that a smile given to waiters, porters, railway conductors, hotel clerks, and shopkeepers, worked magic in lands where language was a barrier.

In the present upset condition of the world we shall make little progress toward peace and friendly relations until nations stop scowling at each other and begin to exchange friendly smiles. And that will come when they stop trying so hard to *get,* and do a little *giving.*

Some place, years ago, I encountered a legend that I have never forgotten: "Good nature begets smiles, smiles beget friends, and friends are better than a fortune."

◆   ◆   ◆

Perhaps you have never thought of the simple things mentioned in this chapter as gifts. That is our trouble: we think of a gift as something that can be bought, something material that can be seen and handled. Whereas the heart has its own method of weighing and measuring, and its own scale of values.

# Chapter 11

# The priceless gift of tolerance

❡ When he was president of Harvard, Dr. Charles W. Eliot delivered a lecture* in which he made this statement: "An honorable man must be generous, and I do not mean generous with money only. I mean generous in his judgments of men and women."

This all sums up in a single word—*tolerance*.

Of all the gifts we can bestow on our friends and neighbors, and upon every person we encounter in our daily goings and comings, none is perhaps so rare as the gift of tolerance. It is as easy to be intolerant, critical, faultfinding, toward people as it is difficult to be fair and tolerant.

Nevertheless, any of us can make tolerance a definite part of our giving-away hobby. To do this calls for joint action of the heart and mind. The heart says, "Wait, before you judge, until you know *why* this person acts or lives as he or she does." The mind sets out to discover what is beneath the surface, and refuses to sit in judgment until all the facts are known.

Were people to know the truth behind our own lives, certainly they would judge us more charitably. If we knew what people say about us, and how unfair many of their judgments

* *The Durable Satisfactions of Life,* published by Thomas Y. Crowell Company.

are, we would be slower to judge others without knowing all that is going on behind the scenes in their lives. Since we do not know, why should we not bestow on them the priceless gift of tolerance, in our thoughts and in talking about them with others, or in listening to others talk about them? It costs us nothing and may be the most wonderful gift we could possibly give them.

❧ ❧ ❧

A man living in a suburb of Boston was for years harshly criticized by his neighbors for attitudes and actions which certainly were hard to condone. He was tolerated socially only because of his charming wife. She was accepted by everyone, and had the sympathy of the entire community because she had to live with such a husband—a boorish, unsociable man who drank too much.

Quite suddenly one day the couple moved away, without even leaving an address with their friends. At a neighborhood bridge party the evening following their departure the unpopular husband received a particularly vicious tearing apart. It was just like him to go off without even saying good-bye. Everybody agreed that it was good riddance to the community, except that his attractive wife would be greatly missed.

Only one person in the neighborhood, a quiet young lawyer, had always declined to be drawn into these discussions, and this evening he kept noticeably aloof from the conversation. Suddenly one of the most outspoken of the women turned on him. "Bradley," she snapped, "you'd think from the way you've never said a word when we've discussed Jim So-and-So that you approve of him."

"I'm afraid I do," he replied. "More, at least, than I approve the way we have torn him apart all these years. Have we ever asked ourselves *why* he has acted as he has? What have we really *known* about his life?"

The prompt and rather ill-natured consensus was that they had known "plenty." The attitude of the lawyer was resented.

He waited for the fire of their spite to die down. Then he said quietly, "I learned in law school not to form judgments until I had the facts. It took me a long time to get the facts in this case, and I've had to keep them to myself until tonight. But now that these people have moved away I'd better let you have them, as I got them from a lawyer friend who works for a Boston detective agency.

"The gracious wife of our unpopular departed neighbor is a confirmed kleptomaniac. She has been caught shoplifting in every large store in the city. Her husband managed to keep her out of jail, usually at a heavy price. He nearly went to jail on one occasion by drawing suspicion to himself. He dreaded to have parties at his house because his wife has been known to steal things from her guests." (Two women in the group exchanged startled glances with their husbands.) "And he has tried to keep her from coming to our parties whenever he could because she has been known to take things from other guests' handbags."

The whole group gasped.

It was this experience that really taught me tolerance — to reserve judgment on people until I had the facts — and, meanwhile, to try to like them.

I once read a Sioux Indian's prayer which impressed me

deeply: "Great Spirit, help me never to judge another until I have walked two weeks in his moccasins."

◀   ◀   ◀

Probably the most precious thing a man or woman can possess is a good name. The curious part of it is, scarcely a day passes that you do not have an opportunity to give someone a good name.

Any time you find yourself in a group of people who are talking about a friend or neighbor or fellow worker, if someone starts to disparage, you can so easily say something kind, or at least tolerant. It is surprising how often this will cause another to speak up and add something favorable to what you have said. Many a time the conversation will end by giving a good name to the person under discussion. When this happens everybody in the group feels better.

Is there not the best authority in the world for tolerance? The Bible says: "Judge not, and ye shall not be judged: condemn not, and ye shall not be condemned: forgive, and ye shall be forgiven."

# Chapter 12

# Four-cent giving

❡ For four cents the United States Government will co-operate with you wholeheartedly in one of the simplest and most acceptable forms of giving yourself.

All you have to do is write a note to a friend or acquaintance (or even a stranger) expressing interest, friendship, sympathy, congratulations, commendation, good will or good wishes, seal it up in an envelope, address it, stick a four-cent stamp on it, and drop it in the nearest mailbox.

Indeed, the Post Office Department will co-operate with you for even less: a post card can carry a wealth of warmth and friendship!

We fail to make greater use of this governmental partnership-in-giving, not because we are unaware of its possibilities, but because we are thoughtless. We know how much we appreciate notes from friends, but we do not stop often enough to think how much they would appreciate notes from us.

Or perhaps it is procrastination. We promise ourselves on many occasions to write to people, to tell them of our pleasure in something they have done, or some honor that has come to them, or to express sympathy for a sorrow. We keep putting it off until some morning we say to ourselves, "Well, it's too late now. I'm sorry I didn't do it when I first thought of it."

Which is just another argument for acting on impulse in giving ourselves.

❡     ❡     ❡

There is something peculiarly *you* in the letter or note you write. It says, "I think enough of you to take the trouble to sit down and try to put into words the feeling I have toward you."

It matters not whether you have the gift of expression. If you say what is in your heart, the words won't matter. And who knows, your letter may arrive at a time of crisis. The course of many a person's life has been changed by a letter received in the morning mail.

Four pennies is a small investment to make in giving ourselves to our friends, or to win the friendship of strangers who have done something which earns our gratitude or approval.

# Chapter 13

# On lowering the one-in-ten average

❡ Though the term "giving thanks" has been in use for centuries, we seem not to think of thanks as a gift. Yet it is a gift, for every time you give thanks you give the warmth of your heart.

I have had people thank me for little thoughtfulnesses with such genuine gratitude in their voices that it has warmed me to the marrow of my bones. Undoubtedly you have had the same experience. Yet how often do we give others all the happiness we might for the things they do for us?

To realize how short we are falling we have only to note the number of times we feel that the thoughtful things we do for other people do not receive quite the thanks we anticipated.

Our thoughtlessness cannot be blamed entirely on our busy age. It is as old as humanity. Christ encountered it in His day. We read in Luke's Gospel:

And it came to pass, as he went to Jerusalem, that he passed through the midst of Samaria and Galilee.

And as he entered into a certain village, there met him ten men that were lepers, which stood afar off:

And they lifted up their voices, and said, Jesus, Master, have mercy on us.

And when he saw them, he said unto them, Go show yourselves unto the priests. And it came to pass, that, as they went, they were cleansed.

And one of them, when he saw that he was healed, turned back, and with a loud voice glorified God,

And fell down on his face at his feet, giving him thanks: and he was a Samaritan.

And Jesus answering said, Were there not ten cleansed? but where are the nine?

Only one in ten returned to give thanks in Christ's day. Today's average would not be much better. Surely, each of us can do his part to raise this average.

⁋     ⁋     ⁋

One of my neighbors suffered the loss of a child. The mortician who was called in went so far out of his way in the thoughtful things he did that, upon receiving his bill, my neighbor and his wife called on him to thank him for his many kindnesses, and to ask if he felt sure he had charged enough to cover all his time and trouble.

The mortician assured them that the bill was adequate. He told them that as a young man he had aspired to be a doctor, but had lacked the money for the years of necessary education.

"So I decided on my present profession, and made up my mind to put myself as wholeheartedly into my service as though I were a great physician, motivated by a genuine love for humanity," he explained. "This has been my guiding philosophy for more than twenty years, yet you good people are the first ones ever to call on me and thank me. Need I tell you that you have paid your bill doubly by your kindness?"

I like to think of "Thank you" as a tiny gift-token which can be used to make the giving of anything a *two-way* transaction, enjoyable to the original giver and the thanks-giver.

Also, I try to remember that money alone cannot pay for especially cheerful or efficient service, or for a particularly fine job of work. The person who serves us superlatively gives us something of himself, over and above the actual requirements of his job or profession. If we would square the account, we must in return give something of ourselves.

◄    ◄    ◄

None of us is ever too busy to pay his way. It takes only a few seconds to say a heart-warming "Thank you." Probably no American of modern times lived a more hurried or hectic life than Theodore Roosevelt. Yet even on political campaign trips, when in the hustle and bustle he might have been excused from thinking of other people, it was his custom as he left his private train to stop and thank the engineer and fireman for a safe and comfortable trip. It took but a fraction of a minute of his time, but he had two more friends for the rest of his life.

"Good politics," you may say. But good living too—for after all, isn't having friends the basis of happy living, as well as of successful politics?

Nor have I found any situation in which thanks cannot be given. You can thank even total strangers with a nod of the head, a gesture of the hand, a grateful glance—in jostling street crowds, in swaying subway trains, at the theatre, in the quiet of a church service, anywhere at all, if your heart is saying "Thank you."

48

Isn't it time we *did* something about the inexcusable one-in-ten average of people who return to give thanks? Wouldn't you like to be one of a million volunteers to set out in serious fashion to better this average?.

# Chapter 14

# Little sparks of appreciation

❦ Life would be much more exciting if each of us left a trail of "little sparks of appreciation" along our way.

Your wife makes a tasty omelette. Do you tell her how good it is? She may tire of making omelettes, but she will never tire of sincere compliments. What is more, she will enjoy making the next omelette.

One of your children gets a good mark on an examination. Do you show your appreciation by sitting down with the youngster and going over the paper, expressing your pleasure over each right answer? Nothing pleases children more than this kind of parental interest and approval.

You enjoy your dinner in a restaurant. Do you tell the waiter so? He gets terribly tired of serving food all day to people who seem to get no special pleasure out of their meals. A word of appreciation will add a touch of dignity to his job.

A salesgirl shows you unusual courtesy, or is particularly patient in serving you. Do you mention it appreciatively? Her feet probably hurt, and her spirit may be low. Certainly she is weary of waiting on people who treat her as part of the store's equipment.

Your pastor preaches a particularly fine sermon. Do you

take a minute to go up to him after the service and express your enjoyment? Every minister, lecturer and public speaker knows the discouragement of pouring himself out to an audience, and not receiving a single appreciative comment. It is not necessary even to wait until afterward to make your appreciation felt. The "dead-pan" expression of audiences is the despair of public speakers. A single "appreciative face" stands out and is a source of inspiration.

In the early days of radio, when performers worked in silent studios, many of them found it impossible to give good performances. Studio audiences were introduced—and stage managed—to supply the appreciation which is essential even to professional entertainers.

◆   ◆   ◆

What applies to professionals applies doubly to workers in offices, stores, factories or studios. In our working relations we should try to remember that the girl at the next counter, the man at the next bench or machine, the person at the adjoining desk or in the next office, is a human being first of all, and after that a salesperson, machinist, cost accountant, or department head. And all human beings hunger for appreciation.

Leaving a friendly trail of little sparks of appreciation is largely a matter of cultivating the habit of reflecting your happiness over everything pleasant that happens to you throughout the day by expressing it to the people around you. It is a heart-warming habit—for them and for you.

# Appreciation-in-depth

**❡** When some people express their appreciation it seems to have a special quality which I have come to think of as *depth*.

At first I thought depth was a matter of sincerity or warmth. But the more I studied the most successful appreciators, the surer I was that neither of these qualities, nor both of them together, fully explained depth.

And then, one day, I saw clearly what it was: their appreciation was always *specific*.

They did not say merely, "I enjoyed your concert." They said, "I enjoyed every number on your program, but *particularly* the Chopin group."

They did not say merely, "I liked your book ever so much." They said, "Your book was so exciting that I couldn't lay it down until I'd finished it, well after midnight."

They did not say merely, "This pie is delicious." They said, "This is a delicious pie — the crust is so flaky."

They did not say merely, "Thank you for the flowers you sent me." They said, "The lovely flowers you sent me blended in so perfectly with my table decorations that several of my guests commented on it."

While general statements of pleasure or appreciation may

cover the etiquette of the situation, they fall far short of the opportunity to give pleasure. They are lacking in depth of thought; they reveal no discrimination.

I had always thought my expressions of appreciation adequate until I made this discovery. Then I realized how shallow they had been, and how unsatisfying to the recipients.

◀ ◀ ◀

You may be a natural appreciator-in-depth. If you are not, I promise that if you will begin to seek out the specific you will not only find that your appreciation is received with greater pleasure; you will get greater enjoyment yourself from the things you are appreciating—for you will be exercising greater discrimination in analyzing and evaluating them.

After all, if we appreciate something, it is usually for a specific reason. If we train ourselves to analyze the reason, we have the basis for appreciation-in-depth.

◀ ◀ ◀

Still another virtue of being specific is illustrated by the experience of a now-famous woman writer. One morning she received a letter from a stranger telling her how much she had enjoyed the author's story in a current magazine. The letter went on to tell just what parts of the story had proved especially interesting.

This letter happened to arrive in the same mail which brought back one of the author's stories from another magazine with a rejection slip. As balm to her depressed spirits, a few hours later she got out the note of appreciation and reread it. Suddenly she saw that the things singled out for favorable comment in her published story were missing in the one that had been rejected. She sat right down and rewrote the story, and had the pleasure, a few weeks later, of selling it—to the very magazine which had originally returned it.

The *specific* gives people something to work on.

❧ ❧ ❧

But mark this: appreciation must be sincere to be acceptable. We usually know when something we do merits approval or compliment, and we are suspicious of people who praise us undeservedly. A specific comment shows the recipient that we have given thought to what we say, but by the same token it is the more transparent if not honest.

# Chapter 16

# Are you a "noticer"?

℄ A seriously neglected aspect of the art of appreciation is the habit of *noticing*.

All of us put much thought into selecting our clothes, laying out and caring for our gardens, decorating our homes and adding to their furnishings, training our children, planning menus for our meals, polishing our cars, and all the other day-to-day activities of living. One of the minor disappointments of life is that our family, friends and neighbors are prone to take for granted all our thought and pains; they so seldom seem to *notice*.

When someone does notice, and speaks admiringly of our efforts, it pleases us inordinately. And is that not a fine gift—inordinate pleasure?

◂ ◂ ◂

Merchants and businessmen give much thought to the products and services they offer the public. They plan with great care their advertising, their window displays, their packages, their catalogs and sales literature, the layout of their offices, the lighting and sanitation of their factories. It is disappointing to them that ninety-eight people out of a hundred seemingly fail to notice what they have done, let alone speak any word of appreciation.

In taking for granted all of this care and thought, you and I are shortchanging the merchants and businessmen who serve us — and ourselves as well.

Several years ago as I slipped into my berth on a train one night, I noticed that it was made up with soft rose-colored blankets not unlike those on my bed at home.

"This indeed deserves an expression of appreciation," I told myself. Upon my return home I wrote a note to the president of the Pullman Company in which I said:

> I want to register my enthusiastic appreciation for the new soft blankets you are now using in your sleeping cars. They are a most welcome change from the heavy board-like blankets that have been used on Pullman berths all these years.
>
> Since I travel about a week each month, you can appreciate that I am delighted to have these more homelike blankets to spread over me when I go to bed on the train.

A few days later I received a friendly letter from the Pullman president thanking me earnestly for my note, and going on with three paragraphs of interesting facts about "Pullman housekeeping." It was a heart-warming exchange of correspondence.

◗    ◗    ◗

If you cultivate the habit of noticing — and speaking of — all sorts of little things, you soon begin to earn an unexpected double dividend on your giving: you become more *alert* to the life that is going on around you. You seem somehow to *savor* it more, to enjoy its spirit and color and variety. Not

only that; you get a reputation for being a person of discrimination — which you actually become because you are
constantly exercising your powers of observation and appreciation.

A good "noticer" is indeed a great pleasure-giver.

# Chapter 17

# Experiments in interest-giving

❡ In my hobby of collecting practically costless ways of giving, I tried an experiment one evening.

My wife and I were invited to dinner at the home of a man whose hobby is collecting postage stamps. I had always been bored with stamp collections, and I rather dreaded it when my host said after dinner, "Would you be interested in seeing my stamp collection?"

Then this thought flashed into my mind, "Well, I've got to see it anyway. Why not try giving him the pleasure of having a really *interested* listener?"

"I would," I said, and I really meant it, for I was going to practice my hobby while he indulged his.

So, instead of merely paying polite attention, while devoutly hoping our hostess would come to the rescue by suggesting a game of bridge, I got into the spirit of his hobby. It did not take him long to realize, from the look in my eyes and the questions I asked, that I was genuinely interested. Drawing on his broad knowledge of stamps and their history and geography, he held me fascinated for more than an hour. I was not half ready to have him stop when his wife did suggest bridge.

I had given my friend the pleasure of showing his stamp collection, and in return he had given me one of the most enjoyable hours I had spent in many months.

That night I came to the conclusion that the reason the world often seems dull and unexciting is because we are so wrapped up in our own narrow interests and prejudices that we resist it when other people try to take us into their lives. Whereas, if we would give them our interest, they would open up realms which would prove fascinating to us.

◄　◄　◄

To realize what an acceptable gift we bestow when we give our close attention and interest to other people's hobbies and experiences, we have only to recall what pleasure we get when we encounter a "good listener" who seems genuinely interested in our travels, our garden, our library; or in being shown our stamps or guns or butterflies, or whatever it is we collect. He makes us relive our experiences enjoyably. We warm up to him and come to look upon him as a true friend.

We may be sure that others will feel the same toward us if we enter their worlds wholeheartedly, instead of merely stepping politely across the threshold, with one eye on the door, ready to back out the minute we decently can.

◄　◄　◄

Since the episode of the stamp collection, I have tried many experiments in interest-giving. One night, traveling from Chicago to Buffalo, I sat in the Pullman smoking-room reading a novel. There was just one other person in the smoking-room, a man who sat looking out of the window into the night, rather glumly, it seemed to me.

"I wonder," I said to myself, "if this man may not be more interesting than the novel I am reading."

I shut the book. "You don't look as though you were enjoying this trip," I said.

"No," he said, scarcely glancing at me. "I get fed up with travel." I thought that was the end of it, that he had slammed the door in my face. But in a few seconds he said, "I'm a traveling engineer."

"What might a traveling engineer be?" I asked.

"A sort of trouble shooter," he explained. "They send me out in the cab when the engineer on a run can't make the time called for on the schedule. Or when they're working out the running time for a new train. I'm rolling practically all the time."

"I'm very much interested," I said. "Tell me more."

He squared around so he was facing me, with one leg up on the leather cushion, and for two hours related his experiences. He told me of wrecks he had been in, and of the unbelievable speeds he had traveled on test runs of locomotives. He was bound for New York where he was scheduled to test, with empty Pullmans, the new articulated roller-bearing Twentieth Century Limited, in anticipation of reducing its running time between New York and Chicago from eighteen to sixteen hours.

When we parted at midnight his face was aglow with pleasure—and so was mine. We had both passed a thoroughly enjoyable evening. I had learned many interesting things about railroads, and have taken greater pleasure in railroad travel ever since. I have a hunch that he has enjoyed his work more since that evening. When we give a fellow man a fresh appreciation of the interest and importance of his job, are we not doing him a fine service?

I did not finish the novel I was reading that night; perhaps I shall never finish it. Only the best novels, I have discovered, are as interesting as the experiences and hobbies of people around us, if we but take the trouble to give them our interest.

# Chapter 18

# The poverty of the wealthy and the loneliness of the great

❡ Money and fame can represent a curious form of poverty — the poverty of the human spirit when left to itself. Neither of these much-sought-after rewards would be of the slightest value to an individual if he were stranded on an uninhabited island in a remote spot in the ocean, or alone in the middle of a great desert.

Money and fame are only wealth in relation to *people*. Yet, oddly enough, they tend to insulate their owners from their fellow human beings.

The very wealthy man soon discovers that so many of those around him are scheming to get some of his money, either for themselves or for some pet cause, that he begins to wonder if he has any true friends, interested in him for himself. It gives him a curious sense of loneliness.

He tries to spend his money to buy the satisfactions of the spirit, but finds that it will purchase few. This is because satisfactions of the spirit do not come from material possessions or from costly living, but from friendly human experiences. And these have to be *given;* seldom can they be *bought.*

One afternoon I drove around a Florida resort in a Ford runabout with a very wealthy man. Someone with little money but a sound knowledge of human nature had given him an inexpensive little gadget that made a saucy bird call when he pulled a string. Every time he did this the pedestrians in our path would scatter. But the bird had such a funny warble, and my millionaire friend wore such a happy grin, that all along the street people turned to laugh and wave to us. We laughed and waved back. We were all friends.

The magic of the gadget was that it broke down the barrier between this man's millions and the world of plain people.

❧ ❧ ❧

The great—whether they be opera stars or movie queens, famous authors or headline comedians, explorers or scientists —often suffer keenly from the insulation of their greatness. They may appear to be utterly self-sufficient, and some of them put on a show of being cynically indifferent to their "fan mail." But they are not; deep down inside most of them love it! The publicity manufactured to build them up does not warm their hearts. What they crave is the spontaneous, human, affectionate appreciation of the people they are trying to please.

None of us can live within ourselves; we must, if we are to be truly happy, have a sense that the world likes us and values what we can do, or appreciates what we have made of ourselves.

August corporation presidents, bankers, lawyers, labor leaders, prize unsolicited expressions of appreciation. I have known prominent businessmen to carry in their pockets for weeks, until they were dog-eared from much handling, letters from strangers in humble walks of life commenting favorably on ideas they have expressed in speeches, or on their corporation policies as set forth in their company's advertisements.

ᖷ     ᖷ     ᖷ

In the realm of politics we are all too ready to criticize our elected representatives and our civil servants when what they do displeases us, but we seldom think to commend them for actions which we approve.

When we write a note of appreciation or commendation to any man or woman in the public eye, we should not expect a reply. Many of these people do not have a secretary; and many of those who do have are so busy that they cannot possibly dictate personal acknowledgments of all the letters they receive. But they appreciate hearing from the public just the same.

And how can you know that your word of appreciation or commendation will not strengthen or encourage some great person at a critical hour in his or her life?

I think often of the loneliness of Abraham Lincoln as he left the battlefield after his Gettysburg address. If only he could have had Mary Raymond Shipman Andrews' beautiful little story, *The Perfect Tribute* (written many years later), to read on the train on his way back to Washington.

We think today that Lincoln must have realized that his words would live in men's hearts; but how could he possibly have known this? After the long, flowery speech of Edward Everett, the orator of the day, which drew thunderous applause from the crowd, his simple speech was received in silence. He could not know that his hearers were so moved by his message that applause would have seemed sacrilege. He could not foresee that his words would one day be cast in imperishable bronze, and be taught every school child in the land. He could not know—because no one told him.

If only some mother had timidly plucked his sleeve as he made his way through the crowd back to the train, and said, "Mr. Lincoln, I have given a son in this war, but your words have healed the ache in my heart."

◀   ◀   ◀

It takes bigness of spirit to praise the great and the successful, instead of envying them.

Says George Matthew Adams: "He who praises another enriches himself far more than he does the one praised. To praise is an investment in happiness. . . . The poorest human being has something to give that the richest could not buy."

# Chapter 19

# The finest heart tonic in the world

❡ Not long after I became interested in giving-away as a hobby, I made a second important discovery. I had heard other men tell about how, at times when they were low in spirit or worried about something, they would sneak out for a golf lesson, or spend an evening going over their fishing gear or fussing with their collection of old firearms, and their spirit would rise. Well, I discovered that if I turned to my new hobby I got the same lift. The reason was, of course, that it took me out of myself.

When you are feeling sorry for yourself, it requires a little more conscious effort to start looking around for some way to give yourself away than it does when you are feeling gay and generous. But it works like magic!

Suppose you wake up grumpy, or actually belligerent — as who doesn't once in a while? You are quite sure that nothing or nobody can make you feel cheerful. You are just in for a "low" day, and that's that.

Then is the time of all times to begin looking for some way to give yourself, not to be goody-goody, but for the completely practical purpose of jockeying yourself into a position where you can't help being happy.

I remember sitting at breakfast one morning at a lunch counter in a restaurant near the South Station in Boston. Having arrived on the sleeper from New York, and been routed out before seven o'clock after a poor night's sleep, I was feeling very sorry for David Dunn.

"What you have to accomplish in Boston today is too important to risk failure just because you feel grumpy," I told myself sternly. "You'd better start giving-away. . . . But how can you give-away sitting on a stool in a row of other grumpy night travelers before seven o'clock in the morning?" I argued with myself.

And then I thought of the salt and pepper! I recalled reading of some woman who said she was sure her husband loved her dearly—but he *never* thought to pass her the salt and pepper. I had noticed ever since how important salt and pepper are to our enjoyment of meals, and how seldom any-one takes the trouble to pass them to us.

I glanced up and down the counter. The only salt and pepper shakers in sight were directly in front of *me*. I had already seasoned my fried eggs, with no thought of my fellow breakfasters. Now, picking up the shakers, I offered them to the man on my right.

"Perhaps you—and some of the other people down the line—can use these," I said.

He thanked me, seasoned his eggs, and passed the shakers on. Every person at the counter used them.

That broke the ice. I got into conversation with my neigh-bor, and the man next to him joined in. Before I knew it everyone at the counter was talking, and presently we were all laughing and joking, eating breakfasts seasoned with salt,

67

pepper and good humor. And I had supplied the seasoning.

By the time I had finished my breakfast I was feeling positively cheerful. My mission in Boston that day worked out better than I had thought possible.

◄  ◄  ◄

Walking down town on an errand one morning, for some silly reason I was feeling out of sorts with the world. "Why not try giving?" I asked myself. I looked around for someone to give to. The only "prospect" in sight was a little girl sitting on the doorstep of the house I was passing. She appeared about as forlorn as I felt.

"That's a *very* pretty red dress you are wearing, young lady," I said.

"Oh, thank you," she said, looking down at her dress, her face lighting up at this surprising comment from a stranger —and a man, at that.

Her face was still alight when I passed her house half an hour later on my way home. "Hello—Man!" she hailed me. I had a new friend. And my little gift of a compliment had lifted both of us out of the dumps.

◄  ◄  ◄

I can claim no scientific basis for the point I now make, but I believe it to be sound: giving-away not only is good for the spirit; it is also a beneficial heart stimulant.

It is my conviction that health is to no small extent conditioned, perhaps even controlled, by the circulation of the blood. That important little circulatory organ located in the left side of the breast is, I believe, influenced to a greater degree than we perhaps realize by that other heart which is described in the dictionary as "the seat of the affections; the emotional nature."

When your emotional nature is stirred by something you do, is it not probable that your heart is actually stimulated, so that it quickens the circulation of your blood and makes you feel alive and full of health?

I know that the little surges of happiness I get out of giving-away suffuse me with a momentary sense of glowing health. I have come to believe that my hobby of giving-away, with the flush of pleasure it brings, is the finest heart tonic in the world!

# Chapter 20

# Giving yourself to a group

❡ One of my friends used to be painfully self-conscious in a group. He dreaded to enter a roomful of people. One day he made the interesting discovery that he could overcome this diffidence by, as he expresses it, "giving myself to the group."

This is his technique: whenever he steps into a room where there are several persons, he glances around to see if there is not something he can do to make someone in the room happier or more comfortable.

For instance, it may be that the sun is shining in someone's eyes. Or there may be no ash tray near someone who is smoking. Or it may be evident that moving a floor lamp will throw a better light over the shoulder of a person who is reading or playing a game. Or perhaps a cocktail glass has been left on the edge of a table where it is sure to be knocked off. Or a lighted cigarette is poised precariously on the rim of an ash tray, ready to fall and burn the table cover. Or he may notice that a chair has been left in a position where people are likely to bump into it.

This man does not make the mistake of rushing to do something about any of these situations. He watches his opportunity quietly to lower the shade a little. He looks around for an unused ash tray and places it beside the smoker, without comment. He moves the floor lamp the necessary inches to throw a better light. He puts the cocktail glass in a safe place. He extinguishes the cigarette. He shifts the chair to make a clear passage. All of these little services he performs unobtrusively as he moves about talking with people.

This man reports that he has found twenty-odd things that can be done to make a group of people more comfortable. Most of them can be managed without anyone noticing—and he is particular about this, for he doesn't want to seem to be a bustling busybody.

"Frequently I get a smile of appreciation," he says, "but my real reward is that my self-consciousness has disappeared. The reason, of course, is that I am no longer thinking of myself."

# Chapter 21

# Citizenship-giving

❧ I have discovered that there are many ways a citizen can give himself to his neighborhood or community, with small expenditure of time or effort.

For example, the traffic light at the top of a certain hill in my neighborhood changed so quickly that if as many as four cars were waiting for the green light, it turned back to red before the fourth car could get through. Everybody was cussing that light, but no one was doing anything about it.

Here was an opportunity to do a bit of citizenship-giving. I wrote a note to the Police Department calling attention to the situation. By the next afternoon the green-light interval had been lengthened.

Another example: One evening at a dinner party someone told the distressing situation of a woman living on one of the heavily traveled streets of our town who was dying of cancer. Every time a heavy truck or bus went over a hump in the macadam pavement in front of her house, the resulting vibration shook her bed and caused her acute pain.

The next morning I called the Commissioner of Streets and explained the situation. Before nightfall a paving crew had leveled that hump. Not only the cancer patient, but all of her neighbors and friends were relieved, for they had suffered for her.

These two experiences taught me this important lesson in community affairs: Never assume that anything wrong has to *stay* that way. It is an old saying that what is everybody's business is nobody's business. Whenever anything in the everybody's-business category comes to my attention, I do whatever I can about it. I have found endless opportunities.

❧   ❧   ❧

Driving to the office one morning, I noticed a metal hoop in the middle of the road. I started to steer around it. Then my impulse-habit prodded me into action. Pulling over to the curb, I got out and picked up the hoop and tossed it into a safe place, before its sharp edge could cut some motorist's tire.

Half an hour later a stranger came up to me in the Post Office. "I just want to say that I wish there were more citizens as thoughtful as you," he said. "I saw you pick up that hoop. After this I'm never going to drive past such hazards. Thanks for waking me up."

That is another fine thing about giving yourself away: you may be starting a chain of giving.

❧   ❧   ❧

Walking along a country road in New England one Sunday morning with a friend, I observed that whenever we came to an unsightly piece of paper, a pasteboard box or a bottle, he would pick it up and toss it over the stone wall, out of sight.

"I appointed myself a Roadside Pickup Committee of One many years ago," this man explained, "and it has been great fun."

I soon found myself clearing one side of the road while he cleared the other. All the rest of the summer, every time I traveled that road, its neatness gave me special pleasure. In my walks in the country I now pick up as I go, and find it makes my strolls more enjoyable.

⌐ ⌐ ⌐

These are all negative examples; but there are plenty of positive ways a citizen of good will can give to his city or town or village.

A printer in a western town was annoyed by the hand-lettered signs in the windows and on the doors of many of the retail stores explaining that they were closed on Wednesday afternoons.

"Those crude signs are a disgrace to this town," he complained to his wife.

"Well," she asked, "why don't you furnish the merchants with neatly printed signs—with your compliments? Wouldn't it be good advertising for you?"

"That's a good idea," he said. The very next day he printed three sizes of "Closed Wednesday Afternoon" signs and sent a set to each merchant, offering to supply, gratis, as many additional sets as might be needed.

He didn't even put his advertisement on the signs. "I don't care whether anybody remembers that I printed them," he told his wife. "I'm getting a kick out of seeing how much I have improved the appearance of the stores of this town!"

The last I heard he was looking for other ways he could use inexpensive forms of printing to dress up the town so that as a printer he could take pride in it. My guess is he has found them, for once you make a hobby of giving yourself to your community, you will almost trip over opportunities.

╺  ╺  ╺

A woman writer in a Southern city was bemoaning the fact that when new people moved into the community it took a long time for anybody to find out anything about them, and even longer for them to begin to feel at home.

"Why don't you introduce them to the town?" her husband asked.

"I would if I knew how," she replied.

A week later an idea came to her. She stopped in to see the editor of the local paper and volunteered to call at the homes of all newcomers and write a few paragraphs about them, to be run in a weekly department, "Introducing Our New Citizens."

The editor agreed enthusiastically. The woman visits each new family, finds out where they come from, the names and ages of their children, what the husband does, their college, church and fraternal affiliations, their hobbies — anything and everything they are willing to tell that will help to introduce them to the community. Probably no feature in the Saturday issue is as popular.

╺  ╺  ╺

I noticed that a commuter living in a Chicago suburb seemed to know everybody on the station platform. During the course of conversation with him one morning he told me that he did know just about everybody in town.

"For years I've made it a point to watch for strange faces and give them a 'good morning,'" he explained, "so they will feel that they know *someone* in their new home town. It has made many fine friends for my wife and me."

I thought of Robert Louis Stevenson's saying, "A friend is a present you give yourself."

◄    ◄    ◄

Then there is the neighborhood aspect of giving to the community.

One night when we lived in a New York suburb my wife and I were feeling lonely. I suggested that we call on some neighbors up the street.

"Oh, they are probably busy with their friends," she objected. "They don't want to be bothered by a lonely couple like us."

"Let's find out," I said, going to the phone.

"Are you folks doing anything special tonight?" I asked.

"George and I have been sitting here feeling terribly lonesome, and wishing there was someone to play bridge with," came the reply.

"Well, there is—will you come to our house, or shall we come to yours?"

I don't know when two lonely couples ever had a more enjoyable evening!

If there were a little blue light over every door, which lit up automatically as a sort of S.O.S. call when the family felt lonely, I wonder if Lonesome Lights wouldn't be burning in half the houses on every street, and half the apartments in every big apartment house, nearly every evening.

◀ ◀ ◀

The late Harry B. Hostetter copied his citizenship-giving hobby from the famous Johnny Appleseed who planted apple trees over a large area many years ago. Hostetter's specialty was planting acorns. He put a handful of them in his pocket whenever he went for a walk, and planted one in any spot where he thought it had a chance to grow and mature.

He got enjoyment from looking at hundreds of oaks which grew from acorns he had planted twenty years before, some of them six inches or more in diameter, and forty feet tall.

This man gave not only to his own generation, but to future generations. And why not? We inherited the fine old trees we enjoy; why shouldn't we pay our debt to our grandfathers by making the world a more beautiful place for our grandchildren?

The world would be a cleaner, safer, happier, more attractive place if each of us were to adopt some citizenship-giving specialty of his own. We would find plenty of opportunity to practice it, for not a city, town or hamlet in the world is as friendly, beautiful or livable as it *might* be.

# Chapter 22

# Are you a credit-giver?

¶ One of the best-liked and most successful men I know has a giving-specialty. He goes out of his way to *give credit*.

In his business he gives credit for every job well done, for every good idea suggested, for particularly prompt service, for a well-written letter, for intelligent handling of a situation. This he does not only directly to the person involved, but in the presence of others whenever possible.

He gives his wife credit, before the children, for the many thoughtful things she does, so that they will acquire the habit of credit-giving. He gives the children credit, in the presence of one another, for anything they do that shows care or thoughtfulness or enterprise.

He gives the maid credit for the tasty dishes she prepares.

In his community he not only writes notes of appreciation to members of the city administration whenever anything they do pleases him, but takes pains to give them credit to his neighbors and friends.

In his church he is constantly on the lookout for some fine piece of work by a committee member, or a thoughtful service someone has performed, to mention it appreciatively, in public if possible.

When asked by one of his less gracious associates whether giving credit did not swell some people's heads, he replied laughingly, "Sure—one in fifty, perhaps. But such people would swell up anyway, and life takes care of swelled heads quite effectively. I'm interested in the other forty-nine."

I've added credit-giving to my collection!

Gifts-of-credit are, I discover, appreciated by everyone, no matter how old or how young, how great or how small. Yet most of us neglect many opportunities to make others experience the warm glow that comes from spoken recognition of the jobs they have done well.

Just another case of too much taking-for-granted.

# Chapter 23

# On the sharing of surpluses

❡ Up to now the giving-away we have discussed has not involved money or material things, beyond a sheet of note paper and a postage stamp, a phone call, or the expenditure of a trifling sum.

There are, however, two or three exceptions to this rule. I believe, for example, that surplus things of all kinds should be shared. If you have more of something than you can presently use — whether it be a barrel of apples or a crate of oranges, more hats than you need, half-worn automobile tires that you will probably never use, a superabundance of flowers or vegetables in your garden — a surplus of anything at all — you will probably get far greater pleasure from sharing it than from hoarding it.

◀    ◀    ◀

Years ago I spent Christmas Day with a bachelor friend in his apartment in Cambridge, Massachusetts. Among his Christmas gifts was a box of a dozen sterling silver teaspoons, sent him by his sister, who knew that he got his own breakfasts and occasionally served a meal to his bachelor cronies.

No sooner had he opened the box of teaspoons than he

went to the cupboard in his kitchenette and got out a dozen silver-plated teaspoons. Calling the janitor's wife, he asked her to come up to the apartment. When she appeared he presented her with the plated teaspoons. She was delighted.

"I might possibly need those spoons—some time," he explained to me, "but I don't need them now—and with her large family she does need them."

This spontaneous action awoke me to a realization that, as far as our happiness is concerned, we are living *now*—not tomorrow or next week or next year. If all of us were to share our present surpluses, we should probably find that our future needs would be taken care of in good time.

◆ ◆ ◆

In the world's attics, basements, cupboards and bureau drawers are millions of dollars' worth of perfectly good things —furniture, clothing, linens, curtains, tools, toys, baby things, luggage, electrical equipment, cooking utensils, porch and garden furniture—just taking up room and collecting dust year after year. They are not serving us, and in most cases might better be given to someone who can use them—now.

One of my neighbors, a widow with a large house furnished to the point of overcrowdedness, recently started to give away everything she is not using. And what joy she is getting out of presenting these things to needy people, young couples just setting up housekeeping, friends, relatives and neighbors!

I watched her as she presented one of her neighbors with a length of garden hose. She did not make the mistake of doing it in a Lady Bountiful spirit.

"I wonder if you can use this section of garden hose," she said. "I have more hose than I can possibly use. When it is coiled up in the garage the coil is so big it's in the way. . . . No; I couldn't think of accepting anything for it. I just want to feel that it is being useful to someone."

⸙ ⸙ ⸙

My Uncle Ed owned an unusual mustache cup and saucer, designed for use by a left-handed person. Uncle Ed was not interested in collecting mustache cups, so this one was stored in a box in his attic.

For years he tried to sell it to a man who had a very fine collection, but no left-handed ones. The collector, a man of modest means, could not afford the price he asked for it.

"Why don't you give it to him, and have the pleasure of thinking of that cup occupying a place of honor in his collection?" I once asked my uncle.

"Give it to him?" he snorted. "I paid six dollars for it twenty years ago, and it must be worth much more now."

When Uncle Ed was in his last illness he sent for the collector and gave him the cup. "I've hated myself for holding out for my price all these years," he told him. "I realize now that I've been cheating myself as well as you."

This incident reminded me of Axel Munthe's wise observation about money and material things: "What you keep to yourself you lose, what you give away you keep forever."

⸙ ⸙ ⸙

The most individual example of surplus-sharing I have ever encountered was the sharing of a talent. One day I met a well-known author on the street in New York. "What are you writing now?" I asked.

"I'm writing a book for my maiden sister," he replied. "I have enough royalties rolling in to take care of me and my family. So I'm going to assign the royalties on this book, large or small as they may be—to her—though I haven't told her yet. I'm having a grand time working on her surprise book!"

＊　＊　＊

Speaking of books, another minor exception I make to my rule of costless giving is that I often send books to friends. Nor does this violate my philosophy of giving *myself*, for any book that I have discovered and adopted is really part of *me*.

I never like to borrow a book, because if it promises to be useful to me I want to keep it handy for reference. And if it is a book which inspires me, I want to keep it by me to pick up when my spirit needs refreshing. I know that many others have this same feeling, so I do not like to lend books to friends; I nearly always give them, to be kept.

Sometimes I send books to virtual strangers, when I feel sure they will be interested in some "find" I have made. Several wonderful friendships have been started in this way.

＊　＊　＊

Most of us have surpluses of one sort or another which we could share. And after all, as Norma S. Scholl writes, "Everything we have is really *loaned* to us; we can't take anything with us when we depart. If we have no use for a thing, we should pass it on to someone else who can use it—*now*."

83

# Chapter 24

# The gracious art of receiving

❧ In an article in *The Reader's Digest* describing that un-forgettable character, Edward Sheldon, Anne Morrow Lindbergh wrote: "He knew how to receive so graciously that the gift was enhanced by its reception. It was the rarest pleasure to bring things to him. . . . Warmed by his welcome, how beautiful became the things one brought to him."

To be a really successful giver-away it is necessary, also, to study the art of graceful and generous receiving. "To receive a present handsomely and in the right spirit," wrote Leigh Hunt a century ago, "even when you have none to return, is to give one in return."

If you find pleasure in giving, so do others. You have only to stop and think how you feel when your giving is rebuffed or looked upon with suspicion, or when someone is slow to enter into the spirit of it, to realize how important it is to accept quickly and to acknowledge graciously the thoughtfulnesses of others toward you.

The act of giving strikes a tiny spark which, if the receiver is quick to react, starts a fire glowing in two hearts. If the spark is allowed to die, part of the glow is lost to both.

Sincere compliments are among the finest gifts in the

world, the most hungered for and the most appreciated by nearly all of us. Yet how few of us have learned to receive a compliment gracefully. Instead, we too often clumsily bat it back by making an awkward disclaimer which spoils the pleasure for both parties.

Among all of the people I know, I have observed that a young married niece, who goes through life receiving compliments on her prettiness, her talents, her clothes, her children and her home, has most completely mastered the art of receiving compliments, and doing it without the least trace of self-complacency. Giving her a compliment is always an enjoyable experience.

A study of her technique reveals it to be simple indeed. First, a quick smile of appreciation. Then an equally quick "Thank you," followed by some phrase that takes the spotlight off herself. For example, "Yes, *isn't* it a pretty dress. Mother sent it to me." Or, "I got the idea for rearranging the room from So-and-So's new book on interior decorating."

Her secret is that she never keeps compliments to herself, though she admits that she "thrives on them." She accepts them for a fleeting second—and then passes them on.

Whether we are giving compliments or sharing surpluses, all of us like our gifts to be received graciously, but not selfishly. Again my attractive niece provides the pattern. She is as generous in giving compliments to others as she is gracious in receiving them. While she never makes the mistake of trying to pass a compliment right back, on a clumsy *quid-pro-quo* basis, she does watch for a later opportunity to return it, when it will not seem like barter. She believes in keeping her Compliment Account balanced.

Receiving, like giving, must be kept *fresh*. All the fun is killed for the giver if his or her gift is taken for granted. The fact that I have received the same kind of a gift from a person before, does not entitle me to assume that my appreciation is understood and need not be expressed again. It is my feeling that we have no right to take for granted that even members of our family know that we appreciate the things they give us or do for us, no matter how often repeated. All of us like to be *told* that our gifts-of-ourselves are appreciated.

◄   ◄   ◄

A little touch of ceremony is never amiss in connection with giving and receiving, no matter how simple the gift or how expected. I know an elderly gentleman who goes out to the garden every summer morning, picks a single bloom of whatever is in flower, and takes it to his invalid wife. The smile on her face as he presents it to her, and her exclamation of pleasure, are so genuine that an outsider would assume this was the first such attention she had ever received; yet the little ceremony is thirty summers old.

◄   ◄   ◄

Years ago I learned that a "second thanks" is an important part of the gracious art of receiving. If a person sends me a book and I cannot read it immediately, I write a note of appreciation at the time. Later — and it may be many months, for I have much reading to do — when I finish the book I write a second note, telling the giver of my enjoyment, this time in specific terms.

Recently I had the pleasure of being on the receiving

end of a "second thanks." Four years ago I gave one of my nephews a metallurgical handbook as a birthday present, for which he thanked me appropriately at the time. Recently I received a letter from him saying that he had changed his job, and that in his new work he had occasion to refer almost daily to the handbook I had given him. He wanted me to know how useful my gift was proving.

This note made so favorable an impression on me that I now have my eye peeled for other books to send this appreciative young man.

◂  ◂  ◂

The "second thanks" idea is by no means confined to gifts of books. It is as broad as giving and receiving. And here, again, acting on impulse helps to make your life much more interesting.

Two years ago a friend sent me an ingenious aluminum lime squeezer. One evening last summer when my family was away I used it to make myself a cool drink. As I sat on the porch sipping the drink, I felt a surge of appreciation for my friend's thoughtfulness in sending me the handy gadget.

"Why not *tell* him?" I asked myself. I went to the phone and called him up.

"I just used that tricky lime squeezer you gave me, to make a cold drink," I said. "I thought I'd call you up and tell you how much I am enjoying that gadget. . . . Yes, my family is away. . . . Yours too? *Well, come on over!*"

Ten minutes later John arrived. What had started out to be a lonesome evening for each of us turned into a thoroughly enjoyable one for both of us.

If you were to take stock right now of the nice things that have been given to you, or done for you, for which you have already expressed your appreciation once, you would probably find that you are still enjoying a number of them. If you are not already an habitual "second-thanker," why not take the trouble to tell the givers—again—of your pleasure? They will appreciate it; and you will refresh your own spirit by re-appreciating the gift.

# Chapter 25

# The investment of influence

❡ Years ago Newell Dwight Hillis, then pastor of Plymouth Congregational Church, Brooklyn, wrote a stimulating little book entitled *The Investment of Influence*. It has been out of print for many years, but it has never been out of my mind. Its theme was that every individual is richer and more powerful than he thinks.

Each of us, no matter how humble our situation, has at least a small circle of friends and acquaintances who are influenced, consciously or unconsciously, by our ideas, our example, our character. Daily, in our contacts with them, we are giving ourselves to them, whether we realize it or not.

A small act that costs us little in time or effort may make the day supremely happy for some person in this group. An unconscious giving of ourselves, in tolerance or loyalty, to a friend or neighbor may carry him through a tight place. A word of encouragement from us, at just the right moment, may alter the entire life of someone who looks up to us to an extent we do not realize.

Then there is the matter of "building up" our friends and working associates.

Many years ago Elihu Root wrote: "I observe that there

are two entirely different theories according to which individual men seek to get on in the world. One theory leads a man to pull down everybody around him in order to climb up on them to a higher place. The other leads a man to help everybody around him in order that he may go up with them."

It is so easy to use our influence to pull people down, by belittling their achievements, pointing out their weaknesses (and who of us is without his weaknesses?) and undermining their characters by spreading gossip. In so doing we belittle ourselves, and lose the respect of people who are too big to stoop to such things.

Whereas, when we do everything in our power to build up other people, we build ourselves too, in character, reputation and self-respect.

ㄱ   ㄱ   ㄱ

You and I belong a little to the neighborhood in which we live, a little to our city or town and state, a little to our country, and at least a tiny bit to all humanity.

It is a mistake, therefore, for us to concentrate our influence by too narrowly confining our giving-away, for if we concentrate on family and close friends we are shortchanging the world. Furthermore, we are missing the joy of sharing ourselves broadly, and we are using only a fraction of our giving-muscles.

But perhaps the most important reason for not concentrating our giving-away on a few people is that it tends to make them selfish, which is as great a disservice as one human being can do to others. Not only does it deny them the pleasure of giving themselves, by making them chronic receivers, but it undermines their self-respect.

So, when people grow used to your gifts of yourself and begin to demand them, it is time to stop giving so much to those particular people. This may wake them up to their self-centeredness—and such an awakening is in itself a valuable gift.

Therefore be wise. Spread your giving-away over a constantly widening circle of friends, relatives, business or professional associates, acquaintances, neighbors, yes, and strangers. To do so will extend your influence in an ever-widening circle, enriching the lives of many people.

# Chapter 26

# For teen-agers only

(Parents please keep out)

❧ I have made an interesting discovery about young people. Once they get the idea, they are better givers-away than most grown-ups. Since most of them haven't much money to spend, they have only *themselves* to give. So they think up ways that would never occur to older people, whose ideas about giving usually start with money, or with things that cost money.

Then, too, young people are more impulsive. They have fewer inhibitions; they are less afraid of being snubbed. They think of a nice thing to do for someone — and *do* it. And that is the real secret of being good at giving-away: to act on a generous impulse before it has time to cool.

❧     ❧     ❧

The best place to start your giving is right at home. After all, you are a member of the family, and the more you contribute to its happiness, the better the family will be, and the more fun you will have together.

Being constantly *told* to do things around home is a bore. But it is also the key to some Grade A ideas for giving yourself to your parents. It is only necessary to do — voluntarily

—a lot of the things you know you *ought* to do, or that you are going to *have* to do eventually anyway, to give your parents some "gifts" that will please them more than you can possibly realize.

For instance, you can help, cheerfully, with the housework, weed the garden, mow the lawn, and do many other chores.

You can keep your room picked up (if you don't already) and save your mother much time and energy.

You can do your school homework or your practicing (if you take music lessons) without having to be nagged. (This would be a marvelous "gift" in many a home, for it wears parents out to have to "keep after" their children.)

You can help keep the car washed and polished, so it will be a credit to the family. And you can be thoughtful about asking to use it—for parents have their plans, too.

You can keep sensible night hours, and by so doing relieve your parents of much anxiety—and nothing ages them as fast as anxiety.

You can help with the care of the younger children, so that your mother will be able to rest, or do some of the things she never seems to have time for.

If you don't think of these things as being "gifts" to your parents, it is because you are so full of energy that you don't realize how tired older people get, and how little time they have to do the things they would like to do.

Perhaps none of the things I have mentioned represent your particular opportunities for giving yourself to your family. You know better than I do what you could do to make it a happier family.

It is not the *doing* of these things that is a "gift," so much as it is the promptness and cheerfulness with which you do them. It is the *spirit* in which each member of the family "carries on" that makes home life run smoothly.

◄    ◄    ◄

Teen-agers can give in dozens of ways to their brothers and sisters, as well as to their parents. All they have to do is to think of the kind of things they would appreciate having their brothers and sisters do for them.

In *Your Life,* Marion Simms told the story of a girl who wanted to give her older sister a birthday gift but had no money in her bank. But that didn't stump her. When the sister opened her birthday packages at breakfast, she found an envelope tied with a ribbon. Inside were three colored slips of paper, each with a "gift" neatly printed on it:

> *Good for 2 dish washings.*
> *Good for 2 bed makings.*
> *Good for 2 kitchen floor scrubbings.*

These three presents were among her most welcome birthday surprises.

◄    ◄    ◄

There is one "catch" that may make you hesitate about cheerfully volunteering to do things around the house. Because you are so willing, the family may come to expect you to be available for chores every minute of the time you are home.

As I look back at my own youth, I know I felt that my time was not properly respected by my parents and my older brothers and sisters. Being the youngest of four children, I was constantly being asked to do this or that, often just when I had other plans.

I realize now that part of the fault was my own. Because I put off doing the things I was asked to do, or that I knew very well I should do, I let myself in for being reminded of them—even nagged into doing them—usually at the most inconvenient times. If I had my teens to live over again, I would proposition my parents along this line: "If you will tell me the chores that I am supposed to do as my share of running our home, and I promise to do them without your having to keep after me, may I have the rest of my time to myself?" I believe most parents would be more than happy to make this kind of a bargain.

I would then organize those chores to get them out of the way *fast,* so they wouldn't be hanging over me. But I wouldn't stop there: I would work in little surprise gifts-of-myself to the family as often as possible.

❧    ❧    ❧

You need not limit your giving to your family.

When you have spare time you can offer to run errands or do chores for your neighbors.

At school you can "give" yourself to your teachers, not by bringing apples or being sissy, but by giving your close attention during class, by having your homework ready on time, by being helpful in every way that occurs to you.

You can "give" to your pals by going over their homework with them when there is something they do not under-stand—but never by doing it *for* them.

You can "give" to your Scout Master, your athletic coach, your team mates by acting on every helpful or generous impulse.

❧ ❧ ❧

It is never too early to start giving yourself away. Some time ago a California boy named Jerry wrote me the following letter:

I'm a kid 13 years of age. I wash dishes for my parents in a sandwich shop. When there are no dishes, I grab a *Reader's Digest* and sit down to read. I read your article "Try Giving Yourself Away." I'm not only going to make a *hobby* of giving myself away—I'm going to make it *a part of my life.*

You say take an idea while it's "hot."—"To be successful at it one must act fast, while the impulse is fresh." I got the idea of writing to you this afternoon, I'm writing tonight, 9:30—as "hot" as I can get it!

Starting at thirteen to make giving himself away a part of his life, Jerry will "go places." He will have an interesting life, and make a host of friends. I wish I had started at thirteen, instead of in my late thirties!

❧ ❧ ❧

Every time you give a bit of yourself you plant a little seed of Future Happiness. All the rest of your life these seeds will keep springing up unexpectedly along your path. When you need a friend to give you a lift in some situation, likely as not along will come a person for whom you did something thoughtful when you were a youngster.

Take up giving-away as a hobby while you are young,

and you will have a happy life. What is more, because you do so many thoughtful things on impulse, you will develop a lively and interesting personality — gracious, friendly, and likable.

# Chapter 27

# Concerning rebuffs

¶ People ask me, "Do you never meet with rebuffs in your giving-away?"

Yes; every now and then I receive a snub from someone. Occasionally, too, I encounter a person so cynical that he or she eyes me with suspicion, or rejects my giving entirely.

What of it? We suffer plenty of rebuffs in our *getting*, but we do not stop trying to earn a living on that account. We even expect to have to swallow our pride at times. Why should we not be just as willing to do a bit of pride-swallowing when we are trying to earn happiness for ourselves by *giving*? After all, we work at both for the same ultimate reason — to get enjoyment out of living.

Some people are so selfish, and so lacking in common courtesy, that they resent others who are generous and thoughtful, and willing to give themselves.

One man wrote me, "I couldn't believe at first that you were really sincere in what you tried to do for me. I kept looking for an ulterior motive. But I have come to realize that you were entirely unselfish. I am thoroughly ashamed of my boorish attitude. I am going to try out your philosophy myself. I think maybe you have what I've been looking for all these years — but looking in the wrong direction, I now see."

Some rebuffs are inevitable, and they even have their usefulness. Once you make up your mind to this, your timidity and thin-skinnedness will all but vanish. You will find yourself grinning on those occasions when you bump into a person who meets your giving with suspicion or rudeness. When you reach this point, you will have graduated from the amateur class.

¶     ¶     ¶

Acting on a giving-impulse, a woman in Ohio wrote a letter of appreciation to the author of a book which had deeply moved her. She received no reply and was very much put out. After reading *Try Giving Yourself Away*, she wrote: "I had resolved never to do any more of that sort of letter writing. Most of my efforts have either met with indifference, been laughed at, or were received with a sophistication that merely implied, 'Another scalp.'"

The trouble with this woman is that she has been doing her giving-away in a spirit of barter. Admittedly it is a pleasure to receive a letter in return. But if I receive no reply I do not take it as a rebuff.

Since writers, artists, musicians and stage celebrities are gifted people whose ego feeds on appreciation and applause, I am willing to add my bit of fuel to the flame of their genius, not for their sakes alone, but so that they may be encouraged to give the world still more of themselves. If they write books that give me pleasure, for instance, I want them to write more books, so that I may continue to enjoy their art. All who make life enjoyable should be encouraged.

Having dealt in ideas all my business life, I sometimes try to give manufacturers and merchants ideas for their advertising, for new products, for improving their service. Always I offer them "with no strings attached."

In a few instances my ideas have been accepted in the spirit in which they were offered. But more often I receive a letter of rejection. The first such letter seemed like a slap in the face, until the legal counsel for a large manufacturing concern explained to me that his company received many letters from people suggesting new products, or improvements in old products, or outlining advertising ideas.

"It is rarely that these ideas have not already occurred to someone in our company," he explained, "and if they are good, oftener than not we are working on them. If we express any interest, we are likely to let ourselves in for a claim that we have 'stolen' the correspondent's idea. In several instances we have been sued. So we are obliged, politely but firmly, to decline practically all the ideas that are sent us, even though it seems ungracious."

I could see his point. But I still try to give away business ideas occasionally. And once in a while I have the satisfaction of seeing one used.

❧ ❧ ❧

Nor is the field of ideas the only one in which you will occasionally meet seeming rebuffs. You might just as well make up your mind to it that some of your gifts-of-yourself will fall flat.

So do some of the jokes of even such experienced comedians as Groucho Marx, Edgar Bergen and Bob Hope. But do they give up their radio careers because of that? By no means. Nor do they blame the radio audience. Their attitude is that they have set out to earn their living by entertaining people, and it is up to them to find out how to "put over" their lines. They experiment with tone of voice, emphasis, timing, as well as with the lines themselves.

One evening I was backstage at a performance of a very successful Broadway comedy. At one point all the members of the cast who were not in the scene then being played gathered in the wings and attentively watched and listened. Suddenly the audience burst into a "belly-laugh." The assembled players exchanged delighted glances.

The stage manager explained to me that the particular line which had brought the laugh had of late been failing to "go over." The company had discussed it and decided that the star had unconsciously changed the inflection of a single word, thus altering the whole sense of the line. So this evening he had tried changing the inflection, and their theory had proved correct.

"That's what makes the theatre interesting," explained the stage manager. "If entertaining the public were *too* easy, we'd all get bored!"

Practice, persistence, experimentation are required in any art. The art of giving-away is no exception. If our self-giving were sure-fire with every person and in every situation, it would be too easy to be fun.

A final word of warning: *Don't take your giving-away too seriously.*

Keep your sense of humor in good working order at all times. Add a whimsical touch, or a dash of merriment if you feel a bit self-conscious, or if you half-way anticipate a rebuff. A good-natured laugh is a priceless gift in many a situation. Remember, you are trying to make the world a brighter, merrier, more exciting place. Sanctimoniousness is definitely OUT.

# Chapter 28

# The fun comes from inside

¶ Let me be utterly honest: there are a few people who will *not* find greater happiness in taking up giving-away as a hobby. They will, in fact, scoff at the idea, and make fun of this book.

This will not bother me in the least, any more than I should be bothered if my hobby happened to be collecting Russian icons and some people thought it a silly hobby. We collectors have our fun inside; we are not dependent on the approval of outsiders.

Most of the scoffers will be men and women who are convinced that getting their own way, getting the best of every bargain, getting credit for everything they do, getting ahead at the expense of other people—in short, "getting theirs"—is the only sensible way to go through life.

They are the people who absorb all the compliments you give them, but never give any in return; who always let you reach for the check; who criticize other people yet deeply resent any criticism of themselves; who expect others to go out of their way to do things for them, but never volunteer to do anything in return.

They are the world's absorbers. Their whole philosophy

103

of life is to Get-Get-Get. They do not know the meaning of the word Give.

Such people are apt to discover, too late, that an all-getting life is only *half* living.

◀   ◀   ◀

Then there is the kind of person William Hazlitt described in one of his essays:

There are persons who cannot make friends. Who are they? Those who cannot be friends. It is not the want of understanding or good nature, of entertaining or useful qualities, that you complain of: On the contrary, they have probably many points of attraction; but they have one that neutralizes all these—they care nothing about you, and are neither the better nor worse for what you think of them. They manifest no joy at your approach; and when you leave them it is with a feeling that they can do just as well without you. This is not sullenness, nor indifference, nor absence of mind; but they are intent solely on their own thoughts, and you are merely one of the subjects they exercise them upon. They live in society as in a solitude; and, however their brain works, their pulse beats neither faster nor slower for the common accidents of life.

Such people will not be interested in giving-away as a hobby. They lack the capacity to "glow." Greater happiness cannot be guaranteed them.

◀   ◀   ◀

Finally, there are those who are slow to *believe* what they *know* about life: that it *is* "more blessed to give than to receive." For this group there is hope. Given time, and a bit of experimentation, many of them will work through their skepticism.

The fact is, I do not recommend giving-away as a hobby to anyone who is not prepared to keep at it long enough to discover that the enjoyment is in the giving, and that any return that may come, over and above the inner glow, is in the nature of an extra dividend. Any more than skiing can be recommended as a sport for a person who gives up after the first two or three spills, and is not willing to persevere until that wonderful moment when he suddenly gets the hang of it — and goes skimming down the slope, with the whole wide world seeming to co-operate to give him a thrill!

But of this I am certain: Any person of sincerity and good will, who will persevere in giving himself away more generously than he has ever thought of doing up to this minute, will enjoy a *much* happier life from now on.

# Chapter 29

# Greater happiness—now!

❡ Some wise person has written: "Success is a journey, not a destination. Happiness is to be found along the way, not at the end of the road—for then the journey is over and it is too late. The time for happiness is today, not tomorrow."

If we wait to *arrive* at happiness, we shall be sadly disappointed in life. Happiness must be experienced as we journey, a minute here, an hour there, occasionally a day, once in a long while several days or a week.

But the weeks and days and hours are all made up of minutes, and if we live for happy minutes the hours and days and weeks will take care of themselves. We shall find our road through life a pleasant one, and spend less time worrying about the distant goal.

A stream of happiness-opportunities is flowing past us continuously: during the hours we spend at home; in the office or store or shop where we work; as we walk along the street; as we travel by train or plane or bus—in short, wherever we are and whatever we are doing.

We would do well to adopt this creed, written a century ago by Stephen Grellet: "I expect to pass through this world but once. Any good therefore that I can do, or any kindness that I can show to any fellow creature, let me do it now. Let me not defer or neglect it, for I shall not pass this way again."

◄    ◄    ◄

We permit too many opportunities for happiness to slip by us because we labor under two major delusions.

One of these delusions is that we shall be happy WHEN—

*When* we arrive at a certain destination;
*When* we can be with a certain person or in a certain place;
*When* our schooling is finished;
*When* we get a better job;
*When* we arrive at a certain income;
*When* we are married;
*When* the baby is born;
*When* we recover from our illness;
*When* our bills are all paid;
*When* we own a new car;
*When* we move into a new home;
*When* some disagreeable task is finished;
*When* we are free from some encumbrance.

Doubtless we shall be somewhat happier WHEN—but not as much happier as we think. Life has a way of presenting new complications, and conjuring up new wants, as fast as old ones are satisfied.

The second delusion is that we can buy a ticket, or pay admission, to happiness.

We seem never to learn that wherever we go we take our happiness or unhappiness with us; and that whatever we do, it is how much of *ourselves* we put into the doing which influences our happiness — far more than what the outside world contributes. The only way we can insure our happiness is to train ourselves to be happy *in spite of,* rather than *because of,* what life does to us. When we succeed in doing this we become adult.

❧ ❧ ❧

It is these two delusions which keep us looking *ahead* or *abroad* for happiness, instead of enjoying the small pleasures right around us — *here* and *now.*

My friend Timothy Crowley used to quote a saying taught him in childhood by his mother: "Ye may go forth in search of happiness, but to find it ye must return."

I recall a Sunday afternoon when our nearest neighbors suggested to my wife and me that we go for a ride with them in search of pussy willows.

We started off hopefully to look for these little harbingers of spring. For two hours we rode, every now and then passing an automobile in which we could see bunches of pussy willows. But search as we might, we found none.

Finally, at dusk, we saw a man emerging from a lane carrying an armful. We stopped and questioned him.

He pointed off to the west. "About two miles yonder in the woods, down by the river, I found these," he said. "But you couldn't get in there with your car."

It was growing late. Disappointed, we went home empty handed.

The next morning, looking out of an upstairs window, my wife saw children gathering pussy willows in a far corner of the big vacant lot between our house and our neighbor's

—the very last place in the world we would have thought to look!

When she told me about it that evening I thought of Mother Crowley's "Ye may go forth in search of happiness, but to find it ye must return!"

◀    ◀    ◀

It is never too late, nor is anyone ever too old, to take up giving-away as a hobby. You are probably doing, already, a great many of the things mentioned in this book, and perhaps many others that have not occurred to me. To live a more thrilling life, rich in satisfactions and full of little adventures, you simply begin to look for *more* opportunities to give yourself, to *more* people, in *more* ways, both usual and unusual. At least that is my experience.

Whenever the world grows a bit dull, or I feel low in spirit, I know at once what the trouble is: *I have stopped trying to give myself away*. Instinctively, I look around for some opportunity to share a bit of myself. It seldom takes long to find one. Then I begin to feel alive—to glow with a current of happiness.

As I write this, I clearly realize for the first time that this is what happiness really is—*a current*. It is as though each of us were an electric bulb, some of low wattage, some high, but all of us free to draw a supply of happiness from the world's inexhaustible current. And all of us potential disseminators of light and warmth.

No one has ever learned the secret of continuous happiness. Perhaps we could not stand it. Possibly we should burn out, like a spent light bulb. But I am sure every one of us could stand much more happiness than we do enjoy—without the least danger of burning out!

One thing is certain: When we set out to give ourselves fully and freely, our hearts make direct connection with that great central source of light and power, God, the giver of all good things.

◄ ◄ ◄

"Suppose," a friend asked whimsically, "all of us should suddenly take up your hobby and start 'giving ourselves away' in the fashion you suggest—wouldn't we begin to bump into each other?"

I have asked myself that same question—seriously. And I have come to a definite conclusion: We would suddenly find ourselves living in the most gracious age in the history of the world, with our lives full of delightful little adventures, our days happy and all too short, and the very air we breathe charged with friendliness and good nature!

Wouldn't you like to live in such an age?

Wouldn't the tolerance and understanding and good will that would be generated by such a spirit give you confidence that peace and sanity can be restored to the world?

Isn't this something you and I can do, starting today, toward lifting the blanket of gloom and suspicion that has settled over mankind, while at the same time we earn greater happiness for ourselves—now?

# Some further important discoveries

# Giving Yourself Away

A best seller has chosen to tell us
    How to bring a new zest to each day,
By admixing with life's grubby business
    Just giving ourselves away.
We're told that we all are too given
    To getting as much as we can,
A habit as old, so I gather,
    As this curious creature called man.

But this getting is not all clear profit
    If our natures lose something fine.
It seems there's a law sent from heaven
    Which savors of wisdom Divine,
That in giving ourselves as chance offers
    We shall never lack something to give,
But shall find truer riches increasing
    As by practice we learn how to live.

*B. L. Bruce*

Shortly after *Try Giving Yourself Away* was published, the *Chicago Tribune* made arrangements with the publishers to print a chapter a day over a period of a month. Inspired by these daily installments, a reader of the *Tribune* contributed this inspiring poem to the paper's "Wake of the News" column. It is reproduced on this page with appreciation to the author and the newspaper for gracious permission to share it with the readers of this book.

# A welcome invitation

℘ Some years ago, as stated in the introduction to this little volume, I wrote a brief magazine article entitled *Try Giving Yourself Away* which I later expanded into a book.

This book has since run into twelve printings. Recently the publishers planned a new edition, and invited me to bring it up to date.

"You must have learned some new and helpful things about your giving-away hobby," they said, "which you would like to share with future readers of your book."

"I have," said I, "and I welcome your invitation."

Hence the following chapters, which cover additional discoveries about giving-away which I have made in the intervening years. Some of these discoveries have been the result of my own experience. Others have come from the flood of letters from readers which have poured in on me from all parts of the world. These letters, which I have deeply appreciated, have ranged from a one-line note reading, "Dear Mr. Dunn: *You have another recruit,*" from a man in British Columbia, to letters of several typewritten pages telling the writers' thrilling experiences in giving themselves away. In a few cases they have been from troubled people who have accepted the giving-away philosophy but have not seemed to be able to make it "work" in their own lives.

While all of these letters have been gratefully acknowledged, it has been impossible to reply to some of them in the detail I would have liked. It is my hope that the chapters which follow will answer some of the unanswered questions reflected in my correspondence, as well as serving as the basis for a richer life for those who are already practicing self-giving or who may be adopting its rewarding philosophy for the first time.

To all I extend a warm welcome to a rapidly growing world-wide circle of what one of my correspondents has appropriately christened "Try-Givers."

DAVID DUNN

March, 1956

# Chapter 30

# I discover a soul-satisfying way of life

¶ One of the important discoveries I have made since this book was first published is that what started as a "hobby" to be practiced on the side, as it were, has gradually grown into a deeply satisfying way of life.

As long as I looked upon giving myself away merely as a hobby, while I found life more satisfying I was not getting the most out of living. But as giving-away became a habit rather than a hobby, something happened inside of me. I felt a new sense of human warmth in all my relations with people. Friends and business associates seemed closer to me; neighbors and acquaintances became firm friends; and my first contacts with strangers were often delightful adventures which led to new friendships.

This change took place almost imperceptibly over a period of years. Indeed, I did not fully sense what had happened until one day I received a letter from a friend whom I had once given a lift over a rough spot in his business career. My help had not been in the form of money but of counsel and encouragement. He had written to tell me that the night before he had met a mutual friend at a dinner, and in the course of the evening he had mentioned the help I had once given him.

To which the other had commented, "That man helps everyone."

This was, of course, an extravagant statement, for no one can possibly "help everyone." It did make me realize however, that I had unconsciously developed a helpful *attitude* toward everyone; that without realizing it I had developed the *habit* of looking for ways to give myself to all those whose paths crossed mine.

I mention this incident of the letter with all modesty because it illustrates two important points: First, that in time the practice of giving yourself away becomes second-nature; without any conscious thought you do try to "help everyone." Second, that giving-away is highly contagious. Your example stimulates other people to give themselves, and by so doing makes them happier. In this instance, the friend who wrote me the letter was giving me a "second thanks" for the help I had given him several years before. I am sure he experienced a warm feeling in his own heart as he wrote me that thoughtful letter. I am equally certain that in making so gracious a remark about me, our mutual friend felt a momentary glow. There was, in effect, a three-way exchange of human kindliness.

The story of this little incident will, I hope, explain what I mean by experiencing "a new sense of human warmth in all my relations with people." I found myself sending out little currents of friendship which flowed back to me from the most unexpected directions and at the most unexpected times. Investments I had made in giving-away years and years ago kept returning dividends of happiness to me when my spirit most needed a lift. We just *can't* give ourselves away, selflessly, without getting back far more than we give.

In this matter of bread returning on the waters, one reader of this book took me to task for even mentioning such a possibility. "It takes all of the virtue out of your giving philosophy," he argued.

I cheerfully admitted to this correspondent that to give *expecting* a return is not true giving. But to enjoy the unexpected dividends that come to one along the way is to honor the philosophy, for it means that others are experiencing a happy glow in giving to you. And we should learn to accept graciously just as we must be gracious in our giving-away.

*  *  *

Today I realize that the idea which came to me one night on the Twentieth Century Limited, and evolved into what for a long time I thought of as a hobby, has proved so productive of inner happiness, and so effective in cementing friendships and giving me a greater sense of paying my way in the world (to a very modest extent to be sure), that it has become a soul-satisfying way of life.

Giving-away has become an ingrained habit which I could not break if I would, and which I certainly would not break if I could.

I still meet with occasional rebuffs; and sometimes my motives are misunderstood. I must admit, also, that there are periods when, for several days, I become so preoccupied with my work and my problems that my giving-spirit takes a holiday. Then an awareness comes over me that something is missing in my life, and I realize at once what the trouble is. I begin again to look around me for more opportunities to give myself.

# Chapter 31

# A spirit of good will is the secret

❡ For a long time I tried unsuccessfully to explain to myself what had happened inside of me that had turned my hobby into a habit. Finally I began to analyze the habit.

The secret, I discovered, was a new sense of good will toward everybody.

To start with I had been looking for special little ways to give myself to people. In a manner of speaking I was "pecking" at giving-away. But, like anything else that we persist in doing, this constant watching for opportunities had gradually become part of my philosophy of living—*a spirit of good will toward the world*. No longer did I have to think consciously about giving myself away. It had become second nature. I was instinctively keeping a sharp watch for any little human needs I could fill.

When I discovered that the key to successful giving-away is an active spirit of good will toward *everybody*, I began to experience a keen sense of thoughtfulness, kindliness, friendliness, neighborliness. I began to understand that tolerance is the willingness to make allowances for the human frailties of others, whether members of one's own family, neighbors, friends, fellow workers or strangers. One can hardly cultivate such an attitude without it tending to overflow the narrow confines of one's personality. In so doing it overcomes the one great hurdle to effective giving-away—the hurdle of self-consciousness.

This discovery explained to me why some of the readers of this book who had accepted its philosophy were having trouble making it "work." Their giving-away was self-conscious. Being self-conscious, they were overly sensitive to the reaction of the recipients of their little kindnesses. Quite unconsciously, it led them to expect some sort of thanks or gratitude. If this was not forthcoming, or if they sensed an attitude of suspicion toward their motives, or of cynical indifference, they retreated inside themselves to lick their wounds.

At first I had reacted this way myself to the occasional rebuffs I had received. I felt disappointed in people and was discouraged in my giving-away impulses for days, sometimes weeks.

This self-conscious reaction is not unnatural. Usually it means that, quite unconsciously, we are really thinking of ourselves, and expecting our happiness to come from outside ourselves. Whereas the miracle of happiness must originate within us. As Mother Crowley so truly said, "Ye may go forth in search of happiness, but to find it ye must return." (Turn back to page 108 and reread the pussy willow episode, if you will.)

Actually, we must *lose ourselves* in order to find true and enduring happiness. This means that we must rise above self-consciousness. After all, self-consciousness is just another term for self-centeredness. It means that we are putting *ourselves* first in our thoughts and feelings, and letting everyone else come second. This is not practicing good will, but working for a reward.

There is no self-consciousness in good will. It flows from our hearts, naturally and spontaneously, without calculated forethought. It expresses itself in understanding and tolerance and a desire to share with others without thought of any return.

It was not until I glimpsed this picture that I realized that the trouble was with me, not with the world. I was giving myself with a string of self-consciousness attached. I wanted, if not a reward of gratitude, at least sure-fire acceptance of the gifts of myself, at my own evaluation of them.

"How silly!" I told myself. "Instead of expressing my good will I am expecting my good works to earn a quick and certain reward in the form of smug satisfaction in having done good deeds. I am really trying to *get*, not to *give*."

It was then that I came to realize that giving-away is not merely a series of impulsive acts but a continuing process of sowing seeds of good will.

You will remember Christ's parable of the sower who went forth to sow. Some of his seed fell by the wayside and were devoured by the birds, and some fell in stony places or among thorns which grew up and choked them; but much of it fell on good ground and bore fruit an hundredfold.

It is the same with giving yourself away. Some of the seeds of your good will are bound to fall by the wayside or on stony places—or at least so you will think at the time.

But I have come to see that, just as farming is a way of life, with its sowing in the spring and its reaping in the fall, so must the giver-away sow the furrows of his life with seed-gifts of himself in order to reap a rich harvest of happiness. He must sow, not in terms of *quid pro quo* rewards, but of inner satisfactions today and deeply rewarding friendships and experiences that will bless his later years.

❧ ❧ ❧

My own experience with this little book is illustrative. In writing it I was merely sharing a discovery with the world. It was not until the letters came pouring in on me from every quarter of the globe that I realized what a harvest I had sown.

Three letters in particular have made that harvest richly rewarding. One was from a woman who wrote me that my book, which she had stumbled upon in a critical hour of defeat, had saved her from taking her own life. It had, she said, given her a whole new conception of living, and a philosophy which not only had saved her life but was making it happy and purposeful.

The second letter was from a confirmed alcoholic, who wrote that when Alcoholics Anonymous, which had lifted him out of the gutter, seemed powerless to continue to help him, *Try Giving Yourself Away* had miraculously cured his self-centeredness, and turned his consuming appetite for alcohol into an active desire to give himself in every possible way to everyone around him. He enclosed an expression of appreciation from his wife, thanking me for herself and their four children.

The third letter was from a troubled spirit on the other side of the world who, obviously, had been on the verge of either taking her life or losing her mind, when a friend gave her a copy of *Try Giving Yourself Away*. It had, she said, banished the darkness in her soul and thrown a new light on "the true reason for life." She was making a fresh start, with an exciting new outlook and a deep faith in the power of giving-away to overcome her discouragements and disillusionments.

Curiously enough, my biggest dividend of happiness from the receipt of these three letters, a few months apart, was not the letters themselves. I did feel humbly grateful that sharing my simple discovery had given three tortured souls a new hold on life. But their cumulative effect was to make me say to myself one morning, "There really must be some magic in this little book of yours, David. Perhaps you had better reread it." I did so, and realized at once that I had missed the deeper meaning of giving-away; that it was in truth a way of life. Whereupon I made a fresh start myself, not as one following a hobby but as a sower going forth to sow.

# Chapter 32

# A wonderful journey through life
# on a Happy Road

❦ Recently a friend and I were dining in an ultrafashionable New York hotel. "Look at these people around us," I said. "Undoubtedly they are among the world's most successful 'getters.' Most of them look as though they have plenty of money. Probably many of them occupy high positions in the social world. Tell me, do you see many faces that look really happy?"

We both studied the faces of the people at every table within eye-range. Very few of them looked very happy. Many appeared definitely crabbed and unhappy. At two tables groups were laughing, but it was strained and artificial, not the spontaneous laughter of people in a really happy mood.

My companion turned to me with a pained look. "I don't see three people who look to me to be truly happy," he said.

I was merely calling his attention to something I had been noticing in my travels for two or three years: that as a rule the gathering places of the successful getters are seldom truly happy spots. Too often the gaiety is provided by professional entertainers. The trouble is that so many of the people who are outstandingly successful at getting, and those who frequent these places because they envy the getters and hope by associating with them to pass themselves off as successful, are too self-centered to be truly happy.

There are notable exceptions, of course. Here and there you will see a getting person whose face advertises a happy spirit. When you do, if you watch that person closely you will nearly always find that he is gracious, considerate of the people who are serving him, and more concerned about the happiness and well-being of his companions or associates than he is of his own comfort. Such people are natural sharers, and those around them neither envy nor resent their good fortune, for they are givers as well as getters.

The more I watch the men and women who have been markedly successful in getting, the more I am impressed with the fact that the givers are the genuinely happy people. I am not talking about giving money or material things. Many getters give liberally in this respect. But, as Emerson wrote, "Rings and jewels are not gifts, but apologies for gifts. The only gift is a portion of thyself." There is something about giving ourselves which warms the heart and produces the sensation we call happiness. It also produces a form of wealth —true and lasting friendships—which is more valuable than gold and more permanent than position or fame or power.

❡    ❡    ❡

At first I was inclined to be critical of the confirmed getters, who seem always to think first of *their* interests, *their* pleasure, *their* rights, *their* welfare. But the more I observed them—and tried to give to them a measure of tolerant understanding—the more clearly I came to see that their self-centeredness was not a matter of their own choice.

Some people are born with a tendency to worry; others with a cheerful, optimistic outlook on life. Some people are born with an acquisitive faculty; others with no knack at making money. Some people are born with a love for art, music or poetry; others with no taste for these graces. Just so, some people are born with a giving spirit; others are born with a getting spirit, or else they are raised in an environment where getting is the aim and end of life. In the case of the latter group, it is not their fault; rather it is their misfortune, for unless they take positive steps to overcome it they will lose out on that happiness of spirit which is the finest fruit of living.

When I came to this realization, I began to try especially hard to give of myself to the getters in my circle of friends and acquaintances. Then, one day, it came over me that my motive was not completely unselfish. I was really seeking the satisfaction of showing up the self-centeredness of these people. In a word, I was trying to make them feel ashamed of themselves.

"Certainly that is not the right spirit in which to give to them," I told myself. "Instead of trying to make them happy, I am trying to derive satisfaction for myself on a sort of holier-than-thou basis."

In short, I was being smug; and smugness has no place in anyone's giving-away.

At this juncture I stumbled upon a practical way of giving to the "naturally selfish" people I know. I suggest to them little actions they can take that would be gifts-of-themselves, thus "sampling" the fun of giving away.

For example, one of my self-centered friends made a favorable comment to me about an article written by a mutual friend.

"Why don't you drop him a note and tell him just what you told me?" I asked. He did, and the next time I saw him he beamingly showed me an appreciative note he had received from the man.

On another occasion this friend had received a big box of delicious Temple oranges from a friend in Florida, and he remarked that they would probably spoil before he and his wife could possibly eat all of them. "Why don't you bring a bag of six of those oranges to each of the four people in your office?" I asked him.

The next morning he left four bags of oranges on the front seat of his car in the company's parking lot, and told the four people to pick up the bag with his or her name on it when they went to their own cars in the evening. The next day the atmosphere around his office was so warm and friendly that, very much to my surprise, he called up on the telephone to tell me how appreciative the four recipients had been.

"I've never done anything like that before," he said, "but it certainly made a hit." I told him how happy I was to get his report, and stressed the fact that I had found that sharing one's surpluses was always fun.

This man, whom I had thought of as a confirmed getter, has since become an enthusiastic giver-away. I feel happier to have given him his start than about anything I have done in a long time, for it has started a chain reaction. He is now actively "selling" the giving-away philosophy to his friends, some of whom are as self-centered as he was before he discovered what fun giving could be.

The truth is there are no incurable getters; they are just people who seem to have been born with an abnormally strong instinct for getting. Once they catch the idea and experience the glow of giving-away, their drive—and most of the "natural getters" seem to have a great deal of drive—is channeled into giving themselves, generously and enthusiastically. To their surprise, they have so many more friends, who are ready and anxious to help them, that they become gainers as well as givers.

I am convinced that even the most self-centered people can successfully cultivate giving-away. What is more, once they acquire the habit they may actually get a greater thrill from practicing it than the natural givers-away, for it will be an enjoyable new sensation to them.

To these good people, and to all others who wish to embark on a career of giving themselves away, I can suggest a simple way to begin. It came to me one morning when I was driving over a railroad crossing in New England. As I glanced at the familiar Stop-Look-Listen sign, I told myself: That is a wonderful formula: *Stop* as you rush through life; *Look* for all the friendly, thoughtful, courteous things you can do, and all the little human needs you can fill; *Listen* to people and learn of their hopes and their problems so that you will be able to contribute in little ways to their success and happiness.

Using this simple formula, none of us can help finding plenty of ways to give ourselves.

ᵃ  ᵃ  ᵃ

It takes all kinds of people to make an interesting world, and it takes all kinds of experiences to make an interesting life.

We can never escape from people; and we will never cease having experiences. The art of truly successful living is to mix the people and the experiences which make up our individual lives in such fashion that they produce the greatest possible harvest of happiness, for ourselves and for those around us.

The surest way I know to do this is by giving ourselves away, not just as a hobby—though there is no possible objection to starting it on a hobby basis—but as a day-in-and-day-out way of life. It calls for good will toward everybody with whom we rub elbows—in our family life (where assuredly it should start), in our daily work, even in our fleeting contacts with strangers.

At times it will require all the kindliness, understanding and tolerance we can muster, and a firm determination not to be discouraged by the occasional repulses we will suffer or the times when our giving will be met with suspicion or cynicism. But if we persist in sowing seeds of friendliness, helpfulness and good will all along the way, we will find ourselves traveling a Happy Road in the company of a host of wonderful friends, and hugely enjoying life in spite of its troubles and vicissitudes. What is more, we will be sowing a rich harvest for our later years.